IRISH FOLK HISTORY

Irish Folk History

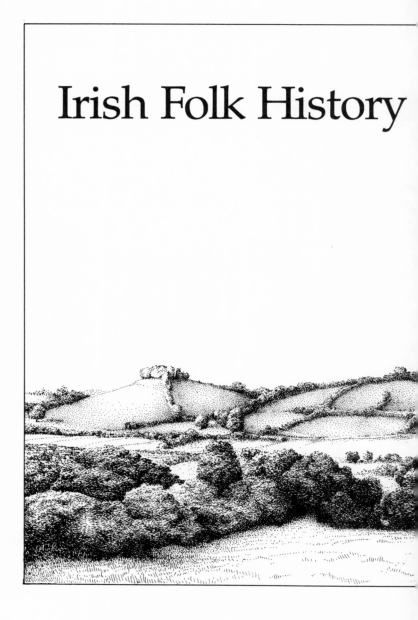

TEXTS FROM THE NORTH

Henry Glassie

Drawings by the Author

THE UNIVERSITY OF PENNSYLVANIA PRESS

PHILADELPHIA • 1982

Library of Congress Cataloging in Publication Data

Glassie, Henry H.
  Irish folk history.

  "Texts . . . selected from Passing the time in Ballymenone : culture and history of an Ulster community, published by the University of Pennsylvania
Press in 1982"—P.
  Includes bibliographical references.
    1.   Tales—Northern Ireland—Ballymenone.
  2.   Legends—Northern Ireland—Ballymenone.
  3.   Folklore—Northern Ireland—Ballymenone.
  4.   Ballymenone (Northern Ireland)—Social life and
customs.   5.   Ballymenone (Northern Ireland)—
History.   I.   Title.
  GR148.B34G55   398.2'09416'13   81-43516
  ISBN 0-8122-7825-9   AACR2

Printed in the United States of America

For the people of Fermanagh

In memory of those who have gone

In celebration of those who remain

CONTENTS

CONTENTS

4. THE PEOPLE

ACKNOWLEDGMENTS

This book is made of the words of the people of County Fermanagh in the southwestern corner of Northern Ireland. Here you will find the history of a small country place as it is told by the people who live there. My first debt is to my teachers in Fermanagh: Bob Armstrong, James Boyle, Johnny Boyle, Michael Boyle, Mr. and Mrs. Gabriel Coyle, Martin Crudden, Mr. and Mrs. Dick Cutler, Ellen Cutler, Mr. and Mrs. John Cutler, John Drumm, Peter and Joseph Flanagan, John Gilleece, Bob Lamb, Mr. and Mrs. Tommy Love, Tommy and Peter Lunny, William Lunny, John Joe Maguire, Owney McBrien, Mr. and Mrs. Paddy McBrien, James McGovern, Rose and Joe Murphy, Hugh Nolan, Mr. and Mrs. John O'Prey, Francis O'Reilly, Mr. and Mrs. Hugh Patrick Owens, Mr. and Mrs. James Owens, James and Annie Owens, Mr. and Mrs. Bobbie Thornton.

The texts in this book were all selected from *Passing the Time in Ballymenone: Culture and History of an Ulster Community*, published by the University of Pennsylvania Press in 1982, and I am grateful to the helpful, talented team the Press assembled around my work, to Maurice English, Malcolm Call, Ingalill Hjelm, Dariel Mayer, Peggy Hoover, and especially my friend John McGuigan. Nanette Moloney McGuigan capably braved the endless task of typing.

The John Simon Guggenheim Memorial Foundation provided funds for my first stay in Fermanagh in 1972. I was lucky to be named consultant to the Ulster-American Folk Park in County Tyrone, and Eric Montgomery and Bob Oliver arranged subsequent trips for me to Northern Ireland.

ACKNOWLEDGMENTS

Members of my family accompanied me on most of my visits to Fermanagh, and they helped me constantly. For his support and love, I dedicated *Passing the Time in Ballymenone* to my father. Polly, Harry, and Lydia sat with me and learned. Kathleen Foster not only heard the old stories at the hearthside, she read my manuscripts, clarified my thought, and brought my life joy.

Help of other kinds was given by Roger Abrahams, Bo Almqvist, Robert Plant Armstrong, Tom Burns, Richard Dorson, E. Estyn Evans, Alan Gailey, Bryan Gallagher, Kenny Goldstein, Dell Hymes, Mary McConnell, Séamas Ó Catháin, P. J. O'Hare, Elliott Oring, Seán Ó Súilleabháin, Teresa Pyott, John Szwed, and George Thompson. And no work of mine can pass without acknowledgment of my great teacher, Fred Kniffen. My deepest thanks to them all.

IRISH FOLK HISTORY

INTRODUCTION

PLACE, PAST AND PRESENT

Dark mountains lie along the western horizon, and the land
falls, soft and green, rippling over little hills. Atop gentle
ridges and around low domes, white houses stand against
the wind from the west. Hedges thick with trees cross the up-
land, colliding and splitting the grassy slopes into meadows
and pastures. To the north, the clay hills descend through
trim gardens on the moss ground and melt into the brown
expanse of the bog. Southward, the land slides along the bot-
toms to the Arney River running east to Upper Lough Erne.
The hills follow, tumbling into the lake, then rising into islands. Around the island-hills of Upper Lough Erne, placid
waters shimmer north, widening, narrowing, encircling the
compact town of Enniskillen, flowing toward the sea beyond
the western mountains.

Here in County Fermanagh, seven miles north and nine
miles east of the border breaking Ireland, people pass their
days, following the cows over the braes, sweeping their kitch-
ens clean, and wielding spades below, turning the moss
ground, stripping the banks of the bog. At last the sky thick-
ens and lowers, night falls, and they walk the deep lanes
searching for neighborly hearths, sparks in the dark, places
to gather with tea and talk in calm scenes called ceilis. By day
and night, people work to build their place on the hills.

Space had been divided and named before their coming,
broken into "townlands." Each townland centers on the up-
land and expands, descending to meet its neighbor in the
dips between the drumlins. Townland names hint of the past.
Drumbargy, they say, means Hill of the Bargains. A fair was

held on Drumbargy Brae in days gone by. Rossdoney means Sunday Point. A church once stood by the Arney in the Point of Rossdoney. Sessiagh was the sixth division, the sixth townland west of Lough Erne, said Michael Boyle, the place of six original settlers, said Hugh Patrick Owens. Townlands give people addresses and identities when traveling, but no single name contains their place. Out of a corner of Rossdoney they have carved Carna Cara, and they have linked Rossdoney with townlands to the north to create an unofficial "district" called Ballymenone, the Place of the River's Mouth, according to the great nineteenth-century scholar, John O'Donovan.

Back and forth across the land, people move to connect the hearths on the hills into "our district of the country," joining Upper Ballymenone (Rossdoney and Drumbargy) westward along the Arney River through Rossawalla and Ross, Drumane and Gortdonaghy, to Sessiagh. Here they dig and visit, forming and reforming their community.

The skies above them bring too much rain. Gray clouds sail east off the ocean, bursting to drench the soil and wreck the farmer's plans. Then the sun cracks the sky, mountains explode on the west, and light dances from field to field, shadowing the hollows, lifting the crouching hills, spattering the green with gleaming homes. Noiseless breezes cross the lake, the waters turn silver, shine, then darken again. Again the winds rise, the rains beat down on the meadows, and farming people learn—as they say—to "live in all seasons." They drop their plans and endure the bad day, planning anew, looking ahead to the good day, remaining alert, flexible, brave.

The land carries their cattle. Small farmers rook the land's abundant grasses with pitchforks, winning hay to sustain their cows over the winter. Big farmers, the minority with more than thirty acres and thirty cows, bale the grass or mow it early for silage. But all live off the cows who live off the

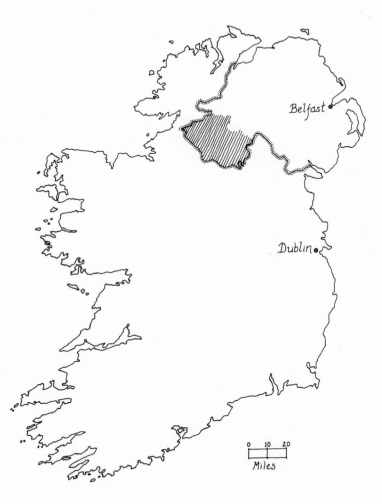

County Fermanagh in Ireland

South Fermanagh and its Region

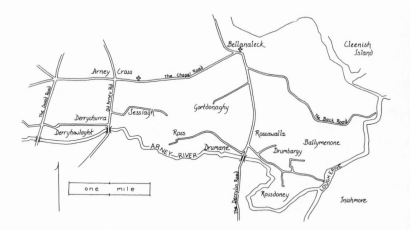

Our District of the Country

4

grass that springs from the clay. Cows make work in every season, on every day, so men's work in the fields, like women's work at the hearth, is continuous, never done.

This is south Fermanagh, a place of intimate spaces and mutable weather, of slow, endless work. And this is Ulster, a place of endless trouble. Beneath the little hills, hideous armored cars scream down the country lanes. The cool, humid air throbs with helicopters and breathes with fear.

It is not possible to forget. The land surrounding every act brings life through work and awareness through history. Piles of gray rock and small, bright wells remember ancient saints. Names on the land—the Ford of Biscuits, the Red Meadow, Lisgoole, Mackan Hill—recall past violence. Cut stone quarried from the landlord's mansion and built into byres for cattle, the decaying house of the bailiff, the hollow homes of dead farmers, abandoned weedy lanes, depressions of old brick ponds, iron roofs instead of thatch, steel cookers instead of smoky turf, poles stalking the hills bearing festoons of black wire—the land vibrates with change, trembles with meaning. When the neighbors gather tonight by the hearth in the kitchen, they will speak of the past to discuss a present too complex, too horrifying, to face directly. They will tell themselves the story of their place, saying what they know to discover what they think.

In the beginning Saint Patrick came, and on the Hill of Slane in Meath he lit a flame. His act, his conquest of darkness, was stressed by Muirchu in the first formal biography of Patrick, written late in the seventh century. Peter Flanagan of Ballymenone told the tale again in 1972: "The Druids at that time said, Extinguish the fire. He said that the fire he lit couldn't be quenched. Of course, he meant, be the fire, the faith." Enlightened, invested with souls, people became responsible, human, and Irish history began when, as Mr. Flanagan continued, Saint Patrick "came from Rome in the year four thirty-two."

Some say Saint Patrick brought fire to the shores of Lough Erne. Others credit saints of the next century, Mogue, Sinell, Naile. But ancient saints did penetrate the wet center of Fermanagh, bringing the Good News and leaving cures for the future to heal the body, prefigure salvation, and prove God's existence.

Since God exists, human beings must answer His commandment to love. Yet even saints fill with fury. Saint Febor blasted the Sillees River for harming her pet deer and destroying her holy books. Once the Sillees ran for the sea, but she cursed it; the river writhed, recoiled, and it flows now into Upper Lough Erne, "good for drowning," said Tommy Love, raised in the Saint's country near Boho, "and bad for fishing." Saint Columcille, deprived of what he thought was rightfully his, a copy of Jerome's second translation of the Psalter, knew rage and brought his countrymen into battle at Cúl Dreimne in the year 561. Upon Columcille Molaise of Devenish laid the dread penance of exile. Saints set the theme of Irish history. The saints oblige people to receive God's word, to love their neighbors, yet the saints were human, they grew angry and waged terrible war. The historians of Fermanagh's hearths tell tales to contemplate conflict.

In August 1594, early in the rising of Ulster's chiefs—called in its day the "worst, most men-devowringe and treasure-consuminge rebellion" Britain had known—the English army marching north to relieve the besieged garrison at Enniskillen was surprised and drubbed in the Arney River. Blood soaked into the fields at the river's edge. Military stores wafted sodden in the river's ford. The Red Meadow and the Ford of Biscuits gained names. Ulster's Nine Years' War ended at Kinsale in 1601, in defeat. The native earls flew to the Con-

INTRODUCTION

tinent, and the North was surveyed and planted with new men. The Plantation of Ulster in 1609 began the era called now the Days of the Landlords. The many endured, denied freedom of worship, trapped on farmland they did not own. The few rebelled. Black Francis, the rapparee, raided Lisgoole. Once Lisgoole was a Franciscan Abbey, but it had been taken as his due portion during the Plantation by Sir John Davies, English lawyer, historian, and poet, first member for Fermanagh to the Irish Parliament. Black Francis was captured and, saying he had "run too fast to run long," he was hanged at Enniskillen in 1782, but his companion Souple Corrigan escaped. Corrigan leapt the river Saint Febor cursed and made his way to America.

On July 13, 1829, in the year of Catholic Emancipation, Protestants marched to commemorate King William's victory at the Boyne. Passing along the Derrylin Road that crosses the Arney River on Drumane Bridge near the Ford of Biscuits, they taunted their Catholic neighbors who met them with pitchforks and scythes on Mackan Hill. Four were killed, all Protestants, all local farmers. Eighteen Catholics were sentenced to death. One, Ignatius MacManus, was hanged. The sentences of the others were commuted to transportation for life to Botany Bay.

In the year after the failed Fenian Rising, Hamilton, the landlord at Swanlinbar, just south of the Fermanagh border, dispatched a crowbar crew to level the Catholic chapel. On August 12, 1868, thousands hosted. They came from Fermanagh, from Cavan and Leitrim, armed with pitchforks and pikes. Mackan Hill loomed in the memory. Orders were reversed, and the chapel at Swanlinbar remains, a symbol of resistance.

One-third of the local population was swept into death or exile by the Famine of 1846 and 1847. Later in the century, hard times came again, and amid them, in 1879, the Land League was founded in Mayo. After long agitation, through a series of laws passed between 1881 and 1903, the League secured ownership of the land for the farming people. Then young men—poets, scholars, and visionary socialists—took over the post office at Dublin in Easter Week of 1916 and proclaimed the Irish Republic. Ireland shuddered with war and civil war, and the Catholic men of Ballymenone aligned on opposite sides of a conflict fought to decide what country they would live in. Upper Ballymenone allied with the rebel Sinn Fein, resisting partition. Lower Ballymenone favored compromise, an end at last to bloodshed. The Old Ballymenone Band that once paraded the country lanes to bring delight into hard lives and provide an emblem of local unity broke into halves.

Ballymenone's history is Ireland's. Telling their own tale, people gain at once a connection to their small place and to their whole nation. Both are sanctified and bloodstained, places to live and love and leave, lands to ponder. The locality, divided like the nation, proves interesting, worth inhabiting and defending. Distinctions between local and national history, between folklore and history, prove false, untenable. A seemingly minor event, the breaking of the Old Ballymenone Band, displayed the impact of large events and dramatically marked a stage in cultural evolution. Now abstract political ideology mattered more than the thick experience of neighborliness, and people "of the one side" split into factions.

That gash in communal tissue was healed by older men who guided the youth into cooperative action. They formed a football team that played in summer and a "mumming squad" that tramped the wintry lanes to perform a drama in the kitchen of every house in the wounded community. Today, though political opinion varies widely, no formal organization separates radical from conservative Catholics. But other kinds of conflict—stranger and native, rich and poor, Protestant and Catholic—endure. Trouble continues, throwing a wild climate around human hopes, and historical stories describe the nature of the community, the little nation within which life takes shape.

To be a community, a social aggregate must have unity. Here unity is not determined by physical form. The community exists on its straggle of damp hills in a perpetual state of negotiation. It shifts and reshapes as people meet, joining for work and gathering at night in ceilis. Kin cannot provide a base for unity. Too many emigrate, and people move frequently within their region. The community of those who stay and endure is not set in social structure but willed out of Christian principle, created and recreated out of the ideal of neighborliness.

To be real, a community exists divided. All men and women, they say, "have their own way of goin on." Personalities and degrees of wealth separate people, and Ulster's tangled webs of tradition named by denomination—Protestant or Catholic—symbolize in story all the community's causes of division. Conflict is inevitable. Eighty percent of the people here are Catholic, but that means twenty percent are Protestant, and people believe one should remain loyal to the faith of birth: "A person should follow his father and be what he was born."

Religion undergirds the neighborly way, holding people together and restraining the power of militant politics. And religion creates the one unalterable division in community, driving people apart and validating their anger. Everyone's life forms between oneness and division, and the historical stories they tell help them understand.

INTRODUCTION

In tales of war, victory is accompanied by defeat. Saint Columcille wins his battle but loses Ireland. Rebels die or go into exile. Black Francis is hanged; Souple Corrigan emigrates. The men of Mackan are victorious, then they are executed or transported. Yet other stories say that defeat is accompanied by victory. People conquer hardship through work. Famine threatens but God sends food. Illness smites but God sends cures. The emigrant shrivels in pain and poverty, then he ascends to new success as an artist. Between victory and defeat, people learn to live in all seasons and "take the rough with the smooth." They "carry on."

Black clouds, swollen with rain, roll over the wind-bent trees. Dry hay lies in peril on the meadows. Neighbors must cooperate in a farming world. Faith is the base of cooperation. Though divided by doctrine, people of both sides share a deep, untroubled belief in God that compels them to neighborly action, to helping others in times of need. Language is the means of cooperation. All speak English. At the end of the last century, less than two percent of the people here spoke Irish. The force of cooperation is language properly used: truth. The lie, Peter Flanagan said, brings destruction upon the soul and "smashes the whole community up." The true word puts one in touch with a deep center within, for truth, they believe, is natural to the human being; it brings the mind and soul into peace. And truth honors the social order; it brings people together. So the central figures in the community are its speakers of truth: minister, priest, teacher, and the few old men they call "historians." The historian's job, said Hugh Nolan, Ballymenone's grand old historian, is "keeping the truth."

History is "men's work," and the men who do that work "gather up" the truth of the past and "tell the whole tale." The local historian's tales fly as sounds out of the dark; they hit the ear, and stick in the mind or vanish. Compared with historical narratives preserved in ink, they are less accurate in some details, more accurate in others. Their authors overturn the norms of historians in other traditions and connect to an ancient and vital Irish idea by ordering history more in space than in time. The local historians may be vague or inaccurate about dates, but they are impeccably precise about locations. Their history is set first in place. It is present, tangible. But they do not neglect time. They are right about sequences, and especially as events approach the present, the local historian's spoken accounts are fuller and more complete than the written record.

To keep the truth and tell the whole tale, the historian uses every good source. Hugh Nolan, who became a historian because he "enjoyed it," learned from reading, but the trouble with books, he said, is that they contain little local history, and the historian's responsibility is intensely local. If he drifts away from home, he snaps free of reliable sources and loses the experience of the repetitious reports that refine his critical faculty. If he attempts to generalize broadly, he falls, like the writers of books, ineluctably into falsehood. Mr. Nolan read, but he learned more from Master Corrigan, a "native of the district" who had received his community's oral history and insinuated it into the curriculum of his little school on Rossdoney Lane. But most of Mr. Nolan's learning came from "listenin to the old people talkin. Well, that's the way I got the grasp of it. That old history is a-talkin as long as I mind. I'd hear the old people talkin and I'd learn that and I'd put in the details along with what I was taught be the Master." The historian listens, weighs, sorts, and artfully creates "stories of history."

The historian's task is double. He shapes truthful narratives out of the collective wisdom, and he preserves intact the works of art composed by the great local "stars." The people who live around him, the people who come to his hearth to sit in the dark and hear, need both. They need to know that local people in the past—the men of Mackan, the Swanlinbar boys—could mass as one and cooperate for the common good, acting anonymously in the name of their place. And they need to know that this place, this clutch of lumpy hills occupied by poor farming people, was the home of brilliant individuals. This was, in Mr. Nolan's words, "a territory of wits." Had conditions been better, these people would have been rich and famous. When transported to Australia, the men of Mackan prospered. Hugh McGiveney lived in the next house east along Rossdoney Lane, past Hugh Nolan's door. McGiveney's brothers became great men in the States. Cramped here on a tiny farm, old Hughie lived poor and died in obscurity. But he was "a wonderful, intelligent man."

From a distance little communities seem homogeneous, even bland, but from the inside they feel diverse and exciting. As stars glitter against the night sky, the community's artists burn away from their darkening contexts. They light the way for their neighbors, making life tolerable for their hardworking fellows. And they provide subjects for historians who create stories of storytellers, factual accounts of past virtue, telling "exploits" that record the courage of the old people, "bids" that recall their quick wit, and "pants" in which their imagination soared into fabulous tall tales. The stars were also poets, the authors of songs, but they were not famed singers. They formed, these old and poor, curious and usually childless men, a special bond with a vigorous young man, who performed their compositions in public. The Irish poets of medieval days had their singers, and so did the poets of south Fermanagh. Terry Maguire sang the songs of Hugh McGiveney. John McCaffrey sang Charlie Farmer.

INTRODUCTION

The historian molds the past for performance in two locations. At home in the neighborly ceili, he repeats the stars' creations to celebrate the local genius and implicitly criticize the conditions that confine brilliant men in penury. And he creates stories of history, ordering them clearly to preserve and present the truth needed by his neighbors who sit quietly and attentively in the dark around him. The public scene is the smoky, rackety, packed public house, where the singer stands out to drive the poet's words through the din. Stories avoid metaphors that gesture cleverly toward falsehood, and they brim with complexity. They give the listener the whole tale, the facts rich and right, then leave him to come to his own conclusions. Songs are not narratives of entire events, but commemorative or satirical, exciting allusions to events. They flurry with rhetoric that grabs the ears of preoccupied drinkers, and they are sharpened ideologically to pierce inattentive minds. While stories use the social unity of the ceili to explore painful, explosive issues, songs assume the social disunity of the pub and use their art to bring people into momentary accord. So Fermanagh's great events are told both in story and in song, and historical understanding unfolds between the intimate hearth and the clattery public house.

The texts—the songs, stories, and spontaneous essays—that follow were selected from *Passing the Time in Ballymenone* so that they could become more generally available. At the back of this book, I have placed brief notes, but for fuller understanding I must refer you to that larger work, where these and other texts are set in the cultural history and historical culture of the people who created them. The stories were recorded at home beside gentle turf fires in a community of forty-two households centered on Upper Ballymenone and Sessiagh, west of Upper Lough Erne in south Fermanagh.

13

INTRODUCTION

Ballymenone's great historians are Hugh Nolan and Michael Boyle, heirs to the legacy of Hugh McGiveney. Hugh Nolan was born on the day after Christmas in 1896, and except for half a year's labor in Scotland, he lived in the brick house his grandfather built in Rossdoney. A poet in his youth when he was famed for great physical strength, a historian in his old age when he was famed for deep religious faith, Mr. Nolan, "a man of iron" who lived like a monk of ancient times, drew his neighbors nightly to the sparkling hearth in his small dark house. His home was one of the community's "ceili houses." There he had learned to pass the time bravely and patiently, but in 1979, fearing he would die alone, he moved to the Old Peoples' Home in Enniskillen. I count it a great honor to have been allowed to spend hundreds of hours at Mr. Nolan's hearth, in the rapture of his elegant mind. Michael Boyle, Hugh Nolan's companion in youth, was raised on Drumbargy Brae, the ridge of clay that lifts above Rossdoney, then slides into Lough Erne. Like Mr. Nolan, Mr. Boyle never married, and he surrendered his life to hard farm work while entertaining those around him with the sad and comical stories of their past. His lungs were ruined during work at the hay in cold, wet weather, and when I met him, Michael Boyle was in the hospital. I taped the tales he told and the songs he recited at his bedside. Mr. Boyle died in January 1974, taking with him the last whispers of hundreds of men and women.

The great historian of Sessiagh, Peter Cassidy, died before I came to Fermanagh, but James Owens and Hugh Patrick Owens had kept the stories of their place. These men, farmers and contemporaries, members of the Owens "clan" of Sessiagh, descendants of Old John of the Ford, live near each other in trim thatched houses. James Owens lives by the roadside with his sister, Annie. Tough Hugh Patrick Owens, who played left forward for the Bellanaleck Gaelic football team for twenty-five years, cut turf for sale in Enniskillen, poured his life into the soil, and when he retired at the age of sixty-five in 1971, he transferred a solid dairy farm of thirty acres to T. P., his son. Hugh Patrick Owens' father, Thomas, served as secretary to the Land League for the School Lands, the estate that included Sessiagh and Ballymenone. Thomas Owens blinded himself with too much reading, and at the end of his life he sat sightless at the hearth composing poetry. Now Hugh Patrick Owens sits in his father's handmade chair, a successful farmer and father, knowledgeable about the long hard history of his locale.

The community's singer is Peter Flanagan. His father, Phil, a tailor and renowned musician, was raised in County Cavan near the Fermanagh border. He moved his family to Kinawley (where Peter was the youngest and best of all the fluters in the marching band), then to Sessiagh, and finally to the house in Drumbargy where Peter and his elder brother, Joseph, lived when I met them in July 1972. Peter, called P, is a farm laborer, a great gardener, a violinist, a master of the flute and tin whistle, an artist courageously comfortable at the dangerous edge. I followed P, my dear friend, to Swanlinbar, called "Swad," where Fermanagh men come for drinks on Sunday nights and the best singers of many small communities—P Flanagan of Ballymenone, Owney McBrien of Killesher, Martin Crudden of Kinawley—assemble to form a regional parliament of artists. Most of the songs in this book were recorded in P's company in the pubs of Swad.

Peter Flanagan is his district's noted public singer, but others sing in ceilis at home. Mr. Flanagan's mother sang at the hearth and so did his brother, Joseph. Born in April 1900, Joe, a sweet and gently witty man, died in December 1979. The Flanagans' house rises midway along Drumbargy Brae.

To the east, toward the Lough, lie the ruins of Michael Boyle's boyhood home. To the west stands the neat, modernized home of Mr. and Mrs. John O'Prey, their daughter, Mary, and her husband, Gabriel Coyle. Mr. O'Prey hails from Swanlinbar and works now on the County's roads while managing their farm. John O'Prey was a creator of comical stories in his youth, hilarious "pants" still told with flair by Hugh Nolan. Mr. O'Prey and Mr. Coyle, who comes from Lurgan and works in a factory near Enniskillen, are both fine singers.

The community's collective voice rises articulately through its individual historians and singers, but I met everyone and there are others you will meet in this book. At Sessiagh's eastern margin, Rose Murphy lives with her son Joseph, a thatcher and talented craftsman, in a house built of local brick by her father and grandfather. Across the bog, atop Gortdonaghy Hill, and next to an ancient rath, stands a beautiful big house. When I first came up Gortdonaghy Lane, it was the home of Ellen Cutler. She was born Doherty in Enniskillen in June 1902, raised near Boho, and at the age of thirty-six she married Billy Cutler and moved into his big house, the center of a prosperous dairy farm where the local Orange Lodge once held its meetings. Billy had died, her two sons had married and moved away, but the neighbors still streamed into her bright kitchen at night. She sat at the upper corner of the hearth, knitting endless pairs of warm socks, serving delicious tea, and delighting the ceiliers with wild humor and spritely tunes played on the mouth organ. Mrs. Cutler broke my heart by dying on the twelfth of July in 1980.

Folklorists come into fragile worlds composed of mortal flesh, of memory and words, and the folklorist's great and primary responsibility is recording exactly, completely, permanently the texts people weave to give their thought and culture presence. Accurate recording is not enough. I listened patiently, waiting to record stories and songs that welled with significance, that held real interest for their performers, and I worked to translate them to the page in a way that would retain some of their flavor. The nature of the spoken tale has been confused by thinking of stories as prose. Stories, Hugh Nolan said, involve the careful selection and linking of words; they are matters of special "discourse" and "line by line" organization. They are not poems, but they are poetic. Inspired by techniques devised to present American Indian myths as verse, I searched for subtle rhythms and attended to silence as well as noise, to pauses as well as words, and listening to the stories over and over while reading my transcriptions, I improved them without altering their words. My goal was to make the texts look like they sound. To that end, I left white space for silence, used italics and capitals for emphasis, and I inserted diamonds (◊) to indicate a chuckle in the voice, a laugh in the tale.

At home and in the public house, in their place of small hills and holy warfare, the people of Fermanagh construct their past, telling the simultaneous story of their community and their nation. Through their history they consider their present so their future can be met with awareness. Between 1972 and 1979, during troubled times, I recorded what they had to say. These are their words. This is how they chose to tell their tale. Listen to the voice of the North.

SAINTS

Soiscél Molaise, the early eleventh-century book-shrine of Saint Molaise. In the sixth century, Molaise founded the monastery on Devenish Island in Lower Lough Erne.

Saint Patrick

HUGH NOLAN

"Well, the principal story that ever I heard related,
    it was when Saint Patrick came to Ireland.
"He landed down south
    and he traveled on towards the north.
"And you'd think for to hear about Saint Patrick that he was just a lonely missioner that landed in this country, and he had nobody *along* with him.
"But he had a very big contingent.
"He had tradesmen of all classes.
"And there was a staff of women for to make vestments (that'd be the robes that the priest would be wearin while he would be sayin the Mass), and for to make all the linens in connection with the altars. He had them.
"And he had men then for makin the altar vessels and everything that was a-wantin.
"And then he had men for lookin after the horses and keepin them shod and keepin them *right*.
"But they traveled on anyway and finally they got as far as Inishmore.
"They come on right up from the south of Ireland and they were travelin through Inishmore on this occasion.
"And didn't the horse that he was ridin upset,
    he slipped and he hurted his back,
    and of course he wasn't able to get up.
"So there was some kind of an herb,
    or something in the grass,
        and Saint Patrick lifted it up
        and he rubbed it to the horse's back,
        and the horse jumped up.

21

"Well for years and years after, there used to come people from all airts and parts where they'd get hurts,

or bruises,

or cuts or anything.

"And there was people, they were the name of Nobles.

"And they were Protestant farmers.

"And it was on *their* land that this herb was.

"And they were all the men that knew it or could point it
out.

"So they used to point it out to these people.

"And they used to apply it.

"So I haven't heard any word now about it this long time,
because the family died out, do ye know, and whether they
bequeathed this knowledge they had to anyone else, I never
heard.

"But they knew it, and they would point it out to you or
me or any other person that was sufferin.

"The herb was known as dho. That was the name of it.

"So then there was other notable things that was, well,
connected to the history of local saints, do ye know, like *wells*
and things like that.

"There's a well, it's above Belcoo; it's between Belcoo and
Garrison. And it was one of these places that was—ah, it was
blessed be a saint.

"I believe Saint Patrick had some connection with it because, I'll tell ye, there was alot of places and they were noted
for what they call, a day's outin. And maybe there'd be a
dance and some terrible function, do ye see, at these places.

"Well, when Saint Patrick came along, he didn't discour-
age the sport or mirth that used to be at these places, but he
made these places holy places, do ye see.

"And then afterward they were visited by pilgrims and
people that was sufferin from illnesses and things like that.

"This sport, do ye see, went on elsewhere or convenient to the place that it used to be in ould times.

"On the fifteenth of August, there bes a big day at Belcoo.

"Well, in olden times that big day used to be at this well that I'm tellin you about. There used to be games and singin and dancin. So this is kept in memory of it."

Saint Naile

PETER FLANAGAN

"There's a cure in Saint Naile's Well.

"If you had any external ailments or warts or growths on your hand, if you'd rub a wee drop of the water to it, and cut the sign of the cross in the name of the Father, Son, and Holy Ghost, your wee warts or lumps or tumors or anything like that would diminish away.

"This is in Kinawley, and the water's risin crystal in under an ivy bush.

"You could go to Kinawley, if you weren't rushed, and you could search and search for quite a long time. Except that someone told you, you couldn't get it atall.

"Well, when I was there last it was invisible nearly, you know. With the growth in the graveyard, the well just disappeared, but if you got down to it, and it's only about the size of that kettle,

it's as clear as crystal.

"It's just boilin up there.

"And it's supposed to cure any external warts or lumps of any kind that would come on your hands.

"Saint Naile, he said he'd leave the cure behind him.

"And he put his hand down like that and he cut the sign

of the cross. The ould tradition says that. And up the spring riz. It says that.

"He says, There's my cure, he says, there for all time.

"The wee well. It's just in under a wee ledge like that. It's limestone rock, though it doesn't appear like high land or anything like that, but it's all limestone around Kinawley. And that's where the good springs comes from in this country, I suppose in your country as well.

"And they say he just cut the sign of the cross, like that, in his old age, when he was about to retire. Of course like every other one, he knew that his time was gettin short.

"And it was said this wee spring, fountain, just sprung up. And there it remained from that day till this.

"Saint Naile.

"That's what tradition tells anyway, that that's how the thing happened.

"And he had performed a few miraculous cures. He had conferred a cure on some invalided people.

"And when he was asked about when he would go,
	will there be cures after him.

"And he stooped down and he cut the sign of the cross. He says, There would, he says.

"And up the wee fountain sprung, and developed into a wee well and there it remains.

"And it's rather peculiar to look at. It's something brighter than water. It seems to be more crystallized or more brighter than ordinary water. Aye. You'd think that there was like lime or some colorin stuff through it, you know. It has a peculiar look off it."

Islands of Saints and Scholars   HUGH NOLAN

"Well then.

"There is certain islands in Lough Erne, and there's a history to them.

"There's an island here beside us, Cleenish they call it; well, there was a monastery on that island.

"Well then, there's another island; it's further down; it's Inishkeen. There was a monastery on that island.

"And then there was another abbey in Derryvullan or Derrybrusk, and that would be in the other side of Lough Erne, along the Dublin Road.

"And there's a very celebrated island down below Enniskillen, Devenish they call it. There was an abbey on Devenish. And the round tower there remains.

"Well then, there's a demesne there as you go to Enniskillen; it's Lisgoole Demesne, and there was a monastery there
          in days gone by.

"It's on this Derrylin Road. When you pass where that military camp was, you'd see piers and a big railin, do ye know, and gates openin into an avenue. That avenue leads to what is known as Lisgoole Abbey.

"It has been gone a long time.

"I'll tell you the time that Lisgoole Abbey went. It was after the Plantation of Ulster, do ye see. Any of these abbeys or monasteries that remained after the Danes, they were taken over and the monks was expelled, and some of them was killed, and some of them died. Their lands were taken over and given to some of these settlers, King James' settlers: Scotch gentry.

25

"Well then, it ceased for to be a religious place. But it bears the name to this day of Lisgoole Abbey.

"There was a graveyard at it.

"And there was a graveyard also in Inish*keen*, across the *Lough* a piece from that.

"And there was a graveyard in Cleenish.

"And most likely that there was a graveyard in Devenish too, if anyone was fit for to point it out."

PETER FLANAGAN

"There was a monastery on Cleenish Island there. They have the stones there yet, and aye the inscriptions on the headstones.

"It is a shame to tell you: I was on the Island workin often and often and yet I never was at where the monastery was.

"There was a Saint Sinell. This chapel down here was dedicated to him. And he traveled—I believe he was a Longford man, the monk or saint that he was: he was a Saint Sinell—he traveled down on foot from the County Longford, on down to Cleenish Island, and that was, I suppose, roughly the most of fifty miles, so it is.

"He traveled down here to Cleenish Island.

"It lasted for over a century, the monastery, till the invaders came in of course, the English, and I think they were responsible for demolishin it, or bringin it to destruction. I think that now."

SAINTS

HUGH NOLAN

"There was many saints in this country.

"Saint Naile must have wrought here. Kinawley Chapel is dedicated to him. He was a Donegal man, like Saint Columcille.

"Well then, there was another saint. There's an order to this day called after him: The Knights of Saint Columbanus. I suppose you have heard of him.

"Well, Saint Columbanus, he was a young fellow that came from the Midlands somewhere; I just don't know what county he belonged to. But there was a monastery and school here on Cleenish Island in them days. And he came to it to learn. And that's where he got his education.

"And when he became a man, do ye see, he became a priest.

"And he was sent away to Europe to convert some of the—Europe, do ye see, they were all pagans in them days and they had no knowledge of Christianity at all. And that's where he spent his life. And he's buried, I believe, in whatever country he converted.

"So he was a youth that came from the Midlands, got the first of his education on Cleenish Island, and after that went to Rome, and then from Rome he was sent to some of these European countries that was pagan for to be converted.

"Do ye see, from the time that Saint Patrick converted the Irish to the Christian faith on till the arrival of the Danes, it was a terror what Irish men, both clerical and lay, that went out through all the world. Well, it was mostly Europe because America wasn't known of, nor Australia wasn't known of, and then for Africa, well, there was very little known about them either, but Europe was a place that was well known. But it was a heathen place, and it was Irish men took the faith to England and to all of Europe."

Saint Febor   HUGH NOLAN

"Well, I'll tell ye.

"That was a woman, a very saintly woman.

"And she was a wonderful writer.

"She wasn't like me; she could spell ◇.

"Well, she had a whole—och, a library just, of books.

"And the way that she used to convey them (I suppose she was travelin on horseback herself):

she had a deer.

"And she had these books in some kind of an article that she used to put them across the deer's back, do ye see.

"So the deer was the same as a *dog* as far as she was concerned.

"The deer used to follow her any place she went. All she had to do was go to this thing, take out a book, or books, if she wanted them.

"But anyway, comin some place about Boho, there was some party put a pack of hounds

on this deer

and hurt it.

"So the deer, for safety, took into the Sillees River to get away from the hounds, do ye see.

"And didn't the books all fall off his back

into the water.

"So.

"She was that much annoyed and heartbroken about the books,

she pronounced a curse on the river.

"And if you'd remark, there's no way you'd see it as well as from Lisgoole Bridge there—if you stood on the bridge and took observation of the river,
                the river is runnin against the hill.
"The river was runnin in another direction, for the *sea*
                at the time that this happened.
"And it turned its course,
        and it's comin now,
            and flowin into Lough Erne,
                convenient to Enniskillen.
"So that's the history of that, as far as I know."

"There was a terrible deal of very rich literature lost because she was a wonderful writer, a wonderful writer.

"It was a rascally act to set the dogs on this deer, do ye see.

"Ah now."

Saint Columcille   HUGH NOLAN

"Columcille.

"Well, do ye see, he was a native of Donegal.

"There's a place in Donegal they call Glencolumcille,
        and I think maybe that's where he's from.
"You see,
        he had to leave this country
            over a book.
"I don't know what's this man's name was,
        but he wrote this religious book.
"(I'm just not well up on this story.)
"And I think that Saint Columcille got the book
        for to read.

"And he took a copy of the book, do ye see.

"So when he was givin back the book, as far as I can remember, he wanted to keep the copy, do ye see, that he had wrote.

"So the man that owned the book, he wouldn't agree to that.

"And they wrangled and wrangled and wrangled for a long time about this.

"So finally the case was referred to the high king.

"There was a king in this country at that time.

"So the way he decided it was:

> that
>> to every cow belongs her *calf*,
> and
>> to every book belongs its *copy*.

"So he give judgment in favor of this man that owned the book.

"So then Saint Columcille, of course, naturally enough, he was vexed.

"And any man would be vexed
> about bein deprived of his own writins
>> and what he considered to be his own.

"So anyway, he decided that he would put it to a battle,
> and whoever would win the battle that
>> this copy of this book would be his.

"So anyway, both men prepared for the battle.

"And there was a day appointed.

"And a battle took place.

"And Saint Columcille's men won the battle.

"And he had to get the copy of the book.

"So whenever it was *over*
> he got sorry for what he done,
>> for puttin it to that fellow.

"And he went to some holy *man*
to get his advice on it.

"And what this man told him was that he'd have to do a little penance for the loss of what life was in the battle, that he'd have to try and convert as many as was killed in this battle.

"So anyway, his sentence was
that he'd have to leave Ireland
for all time
for to never return,
and that he'd have to go to some pagan land
and convert as many to Christianity
as was killed in the battle
that was over the book.

"So anyway, he started.

"And it was in Scotland he landed.

"And he wrought in Scotland till he died
in preachin and convertin.

"All the time that ever he came back to Ireland was—and he had to come back blindfolded because the penance that was left on him was that he'd never see Ireland more and that he'd have to *leave it*.

"So he came back blindfolded on an errand.

"And the errand was:

"There was at a *time* and there was a section of the Irish people used to go about in bands: they were the bards.

"There was an instrument, there are instruments to this day yet in places in Ireland: the harp.

"These ones played on harps and others sang and they went round from one town to another, and noted places like Arney and Derrylin and Enniskillen, and put in nights and amused the *people*.

"So there was some kind of a law that these people were

all going to be banished out of the country.

"So Saint Columcille was informed about it in Scotland that that was comin to pass in Ireland.

"So he came back to Ireland blindfolded.

"And he made an appeal to the authorities
for not to banish these
because he was a lover of music
and stuff like that.

"So that was all the time he got back to Ireland
from he had to leave it.

"So he died in Scotland
at a very big age.

"He was a great, a great man, and wonderful for bringin people to the knowledge of God and Christianity.

"And then he had his own troubles too."

WAR

Saint Michael the Archangel, from the O'Craian tomb
of 1506 in Sligo Abbey.

The Ford of Biscuits JAMES OWENS

"First of all. I heard why it was called the Ford of Biscuits, the battle that was fought there.

"They had a barrel of biscuits.

"And there came a *flood*.

"And it upended the *barrel*,
> and they lost their *biscuits*
> in the *flood*.

"At that battle then, whoever they were fightin now, they *fled*, and it's only about hardly half a mile from this ford to where the *battle* took *place*.

"And this meadow is called the *Red Meadow* from that day to this. And I used to hear tell of the Red Meadow before I knew what it *meant*, do ye see. People would tell you they were workin in the Red Meadow the day.

"Well it twas a battle. And that meadow was supposed to be red with *blood*,
> red with blood,
> and the battle was fought there.

"And that was, I think, in fifteen and ninety-five, I think, that the battle was fought.

"I suppose some of them showed you the meadow."

The Taking of Red Hugh O'Donnell HUGH NOLAN

"You see. The way it was with the Ulster chiefs at that time: the Crown had got into sort of terms with them, and bestowed titles on them, but at the same time, the English had no claim on the nine counties of Ulster. They were ruled be the Irish chiefs.

"But at the same time, they were tryin to work their way to influence—ah, to get control of the whole country.

"Well, Hugh O'Donnell, he was Irish be his father, and he was Scots be the mother. The mother was of the Scotch MacDonnells that had settled down on the east coast of Ulster.

"So.

"*His* idea was,

from he was a very young lad,

for to get the English all shifted

out of Ireland,

out of every part of Ireland.

"The more that his father was an English knight,

he didn't want to follow his father's footsteps atall,

if he could have got on with what he *intended*.

"And the English always had secret agents knockin about, that used to get in to talk with the people and find out the people's minds, and they discovered that this young O'Donnell was goin to be a real rebel and that his enemy was the English government, and the crowned head.

"So anyway, the government came to the conclusion that to catch this fellow when he was young, and keep him in prison for a while, and get him for to take up English ideas, and that'd put this rebel idea out of his *head*.

"So anyway, they put a ship on the ocean, pretendin that they were wine sellers that owned it.

"And they called at every Irish port and made sham sales. Course, they had stocks of wine and they sold it to the people.

"But anyway.

"They wrought on,

and wrought on,

and wrought on,

and wrought on,
till they got to the north of Done*gal*.

"That'd be the furthest point north.

"And the news went out about this company comin around with wines for sale.

"There were a whole lot of people went away to this place where they could be got,
and bought some of the wine and got into the ship,
and was examinin everything.

"And this young O'Donnell.

"The way it was in them days, the sons of these chiefs, they used to be sent to some place when they'd get into their *teens*,
for to be trained to *war*,
and to be good warriors,
and to be not altogether attached
to their own people at *home*.

"So there was other chiefs in Donegal at that time; they were MacSweeneys. And didn't O'Donnell's father send this lad of his to be trained with *them*
to warfare.

"So there was a contingent of them came for to see this ship,
and they had O'Donnell with them.

"And of course O'Donnell, he was a-watchin, the more that he was only gettin out of the boy into the man, he was a-watchin be these English agents.

"And of course there was some of them on this ship *too*, as long as she was at anchor.

"When they got O'Donnell on the ship, there was an *armed guard* occupyin portions of the ship, so they came out and O'Donnell was placed under arrest.

"And the ship set sail and started back
to Dublin.
"And he was lodged in Dublin Garrison.
"So.
"It caused great grief to the father and mother,
and great grief to all the locality where he was known.
"Of course, there was always people knowin he'd be taken out of Dublin Castle, no matter how long he was held in it.
"So he got out one night,
him and two other kinsmen;
they were two of the O'Neills
that was in bondage too.
"They took the mountains.
"There got up a terrible storm,
snow storm.
"So.
"They were followed,
and they were captured
and they were brought back again,
put into the castle,
and O'Donnell was put in chains.
"But anyway after some time, there was a change of lieutenants. The old Lord Lieutenant that had been in Ireland was changed back to England and there was another fellow *appointed.*
"And he was the divil for money.
"And the Irish knew that if he got a good bribe,
he'd let O'Donnell *out.*
"So anyway, there was a good deal of money gathered up. And there was an old fellow that used to go about rivers and places like that and he used to gather up—ah, there was wee valuable pebbles in them days in these rivers, and he

used to gather them up, and he had a terrible go of them.

"He gave *all* to this collection that was for to get Hugh O'Donnell out.

"So anyway.

"Oh, they had a big amount of money anyway, so they presented it to the Lord Lieutenant.

"Oh, he was only too glad to get it.

"So the arrangements was made for O'Donnell's escape.

"And these ones went away.

"And the ould lad joined to count the money he had got.

"Man, he says, this is a great price for a bit of a rope, he says ◊.

"O'Donnell, do ye see, was to get down on a rope, get down on the wall, do ye see.

"There was a fellow came the whole way
> from Ulster
> to Dublin
> to meet him.

"And he was there to accompany him
> till he'd get across the border again
> into Ulster.

"And it was of a Christmas Eve night.

"And it was one of the coldest and stormiest nights that had been for years before it.

"Well, O'Donnell got out *anyway*,
> and him and this lad took the mountains for it.

"So the way it was with the Lord Lieutenant, he had to report this escape, do ye see. *But then*, he delayed reportin till he was of the opinion that these boys was out of reach of being catched.

"So anyway, the storm was so bad that they nearly died.

"But there was a man. He had some job under the crown, but at the same time he was a great friend of the Irish people.

And didn't he get O'Donnell and this friend of his; his men got them in an exhausted state and they were brought to this man's house.

"And his wife knew they were breakin the *law*,

    be having these two boys in the *house*,

    and that they'd have to notify the authorities

        about them bein *there*.

"But these messages had to be carried on foot in them days, and it'd be a very long time from you'd send a message till it would reach its destination.

"So she managed for to get this errand-carrier for to go all the rounds that he possibly *could*,

    the way that he'd be a long time

        gettin to *Dublin*, do ye see,

    that these boys would be gone out of the house

        before the government troops would *land* at it.

"So it was managed anyway.

"So in the long run, O'Donnell got across the border into Ulster

        without bein catched.

"So that was what led up

    to this Siege of Enniskillen.

"He vowed that he'd try and put the English out of the country,

    if he possibly could,

    no matter how long it was.

"So that's what brought about the Battle of the Biscuit Ford."

The Battle of the Biscuit Ford   HUGH NOLAN

"Well, do ye see, in them days, all the part of Ireland that was free from English rule was the province of Ulster.

"That's the nine counties.

"That would be includin the North of Ireland and three of the counties of the Republic:

Donegal, Derry,
Antrim, Down,
Armagh, Monaghan,
Tyrone, Fermanagh, and Cavan.

"That was the Ulster of them days.

"And England wasn't more than a figurehead in Ulster, but they had the rest of Ireland; they were masters of it.

"So they gave some of the Ulster men, they gave them titles like Red Hugh O'Donnell's father, he was Sir Hugh O'Donnell. Well, that was an English title. He was the Earl of Donegal. Do ye see: he was appointed be the Irish clans, but then do ye see, the English king or the English queen, which-ever would be on the throne at that time, do ye see, they gave him and the other Ulster chiefs, they gave him this title, the English title do ye see, that was Earl, but the Irish title was The O'Donnell or The Maguire or The O'Neill.

"Well.

"Hugh O'Donnell, his aim was, from he became a man, was for to clear the English out of Ireland *al*together.

"And above all, he wanted for to hold Ulster in Irish hands. Do ye know what I mean? To not let the English army get control of it like the way that they had control of the rest of the country.

"But the English managed for to get a garrison on the island of Enniskillen, a garrison, a barracks put up there, and put a number of troops into.

"So there was a number of English troops in Enniskillen.

"And Hugh O'Donnell gathered up an army of Ulstermen.

"There was Fermanagh men,
> Tyrone men,
> Donegal men,
> and men from the County Down,
>> in this army of O'Donnell's.

"O'Donnell's mother, do ye see, she was MacDonnell. She was a Scot. And then they had a clan in County Down at that time. And they used to fight side-be-side with the Northern chiefs, with the O'Neills and O'Donnells.

"But anyway, he besieged Enniskillen.

"So there was for ten weeks and none of this garrison could get out.

"They were marooned on the island
> be Irish troops.

"And there was a soldier managed for to get out one night,
> an English soldier.

"And he made his way be boat,
> from Enniskillen to Belturbet.

"And be the time he got to Belturbet, it was ten weeks from the siege started in Enniskillen,
> and they hadn't heard it in Dublin,
> and he got word conveyed to the Lord Lieutenant.

"So there and then the Lord Lieutenant raised an army.

"And he brought all the Irish chiefs through what's now the Republic of Ireland. They had swore allegiance to the Queen, do ye see.

"So anyway, he got them and their supporters into the army.

"Well, this army it was gathered from all over, from the Pale—there was a portion of the present Republic was known in them days as the Pale; it was peopled at the time of the Norman invasion; it was peopled by English—so they and the rest of these chiefs of the South and West, they had joined the Lord Lieutenant's army.

"And their intention was to come on to Enniskillen.

"But Hugh O'Donnell and O'Neill (it wasn't the great Hugh O'Neill, but a brother of his that was in the swim this time) they had couriers all over, watchin the movements of the Lord Lieutenant's army.

"And they knew that they were headin for Enniskillen.

"So O'Donnell and his men started from Enniskillen for to meet them.

"So O'Donnell's army got as far as the Arney.

"And the other ones was comin along, and it was the ould Arney Road. That would be the road that comes up by where Tommy Gilleece lived. That was the way to Enniskillen in them days, and there was no road here.

"They were travelin that road, do ye see, for to get on to Cavan and on to Dublin if possible.

"Hugh O'Donnell had left a force at Enniskillen, and he gathered up this army from Tyrone and Fermanagh and Donegal, do ye see:

   every man, do ye see,
    turned out, do ye see,
     for to stop the Lord Lieutenant's army.

"So, accordin to tradition, they met at Arney Bridge.

"That would be on that road, some distance from Arney *Cross*.

"So of course they couldn't get by O'Donnell's men.

"The Lord Lieutenant's men were stopped.

"And of course when you'd be tryin for to get across any stream, you'll always run along the banks till you come to a narrow spot if you wanted to jump it, do ye see.

"Well, when they were stopped,
at Arney Bridge,
they took to the banks.

"The Lord Lieutenant's men took the south bank of the Arney River, and O'Donnell's men kept on the *other* side.

"So they tried in a couple of places, but they couldn't get over, and they came to this ford at Drumane.

"And the Lord Lieutenant's army, they mustered up,
and made to come across the ford.

"But the other ones *beat* them back.

"And what made things worse, they had their supplies with them,
and all was lost in the River,
and alot of their soldiers killed.

"So they got that bad a beatin,
that they had to turn back
for Cavan again.

"And that was the battle of the Biscuit Ford."

MICHAEL BOYLE

"Well, you see, it was the time that the English occupied the country, occupied Ireland, do ye see.

"Coorse, they occupy it *still* ◊,
they occupy it still.

"But, do ye see, the country was different thattime, do ye see. Do ye see: every county had its own chieftain, do ye see.

"And the name of the chieftains of County Fermanagh, they were the Maguires, the Maguires of Fermanagh. They were the chieftains of Fermanagh for centuries.

"And their possessions, their castle at Enniskillen was occupied by the English, do ye see. They were put out by the English. The English, do ye see, put them out of their home they lived in, and occupied it, do ye see. And occupied it.

"So.

"They laid siege to it.

"The Maguires gathered up their clan, their men, their armies, and they laid siege to Enniskillen Castle to put the British out of it.

"But the English sent a force up from Dublin, do ye see, for to relieve them, for to relieve the garrison; the garrison was under stress, do ye see, and the fort was goin to fall,

Maguire's men was goin to *take* it.

"So this big force was comin—well, a lock of thousands was considered a big force—six or seven thousand men and so many horsemen, do ye see; it was enough to relieve the Enniskillen fort.

"But Maguire and his men didn't wait. They got the dispatch that the force was comin.

"And they didn't wait to let them come as far as Enniskillen.

"They marched out
        and attackted them
            at this ford.

"They marched out of Enniskillen, and they lay in ambush. The whole hills, the whole surroundin country at that time was all wood.

"It was all woodland, do ye see, with big trees.

"And they lay undercover

till they saw the force comin,
and they marched out and they attackted them
at this ford.
"And they defeated them at it.

"And they drowned their whole resource. They had a big
resource, do ye see, alot of provisions and men and every-
thing to relieve the fort, but Maguire's army defeated them.
That's how that ford got its name:
"Béal Átha na mBrioscaí, the Ford of Biscuits.
"The English lost their whole supplies,
their whole stores,
in the river
there.
"They had to retreat and leave them behind them.
"And they were all lost
there.
"And it was christened the Ford of Biscuits,
Béal Átha na mBrioscaí in Irish, in Gaelic.
"But it really is the Ford of Biscuits in the English
translation."

"It twas about fifteen and ninety-eight, ninety-seven or
ninety-eight, some of them. That's the year that the fight took
place, that Béal Átha na mBrioscaí got its name.
"The English came from the Pale. You see there was four
or five counties down around Dublin, and the English settle-
ment in Ireland thattime was driven very small and they occupied just these few counties.
"So this force was comin from the *Pale*. There was a song
made about it, now, but I just wouldn't be able to mind the
song. I had it and I lost it.
"It was made be Hugh McGiveney. Oh, he was a great
wit.

"Well, I only remember just a few words of it. I might know a verse or so here and there.

"There was:

This did enrage
*   and so engage*
*   the gentry of the Pale,*
They sent a force
*   with a great resource*
*   their laws for to prevail.*
Of warlike stores
*   for Lough Erne's shores*
*   but it never passed Drumane* ◊.

"That's part of it.

"And there was another bit that was earlier in it:

"There was a courier sent, do ye see, on horseback to notify Maguire that the force was comin, do ye see.

"And he said:

I saw the plumes
*   of Duke's dragoons*
*   south of Belturbet town.*

"I don't remember any more of it. No. I'll tell ye, there was one time it appeared in the Fermanagh Herald here. And I cut it out to preserve it. And of course changin around from one place to another, it was lost. It was a pity."

Black Francis   HUGH NOLAN

"He was the leader of a highway gang that was in Fermanagh in days gone by.

"The way it was, do ye see, after the Williamite War,

there was alot of the Irish army went away to France.

"And they figured in alot of wars that France had with other European countries.

"And they were known as the *Irish Brigade*.

"But then there was a section of them that didn't leave this country, but they took to the hills.

"And they were called the rapparees.

"And what they followed up was:

    they used to rob the rich,

      and they used to give the money to poor people,

        do ye know.

"So that went on for a length of time.

"And they were in every county in Ireland.

"But this was a part of them was in Fermanagh, and whether this man was O'Brien or not, I just can't remember, but I heard it anyway.

"But there was five of them.

"And there was one fellow,

    he was Corrigan.

"And he was a terrible jump

    or a terrible leap.

"It was supposed that it was Lisgoole Abbey that they were goin to rob this night for some ones that wasn't able to pay their rates, or meet their accounts. And they used to give the money to people like that, do ye see.

"So anyway, there was one of the gang and he insulted a girl that was in this house.

"And this Black Francis bid to have been clear, only for a laceratin that he gave this fellow

    for interferin with this girl.

"He was chastisin this fellow for his bad manners, and for the crime it was for to interfere with a woman-person, do ye see.

"But anyway the word went to Enniskillen.

"And whatever kind of a post—whether it was military or whether it was the revenue men, I can't just tell ye which of the two it was—but they started out, and didn't they get the length of the place before the gang got away.

"Only this Corrigan fellow.

"And this Corrigan fellow leapt the Sillees River.

"So Black Francis and the other ones, they were arrested.

"And there was a death penalty for robbery in them days.

"So anyway these ones were tried, and they were found guilty, and they were executed at Enniskillen, where the technical school is—that was the jail in them days.

"So anyway, the executions took place outside in them days.

"And this Corrigan fellow, he dressed himself up as a woman.

"And he came along.

"And when Black Francis was brought out for to be hanged, whatever way Corrigan managed it, he attracted his attention.

"So he made a very long speech, Black Francis did, about seein his sweetheart, in the crowd, and that he hoped she'd be able for to protect herself.

"Aw, it was a terrible speech. He was a very clever fellow, you know. And it was all on this supposed lady that was in the Gaol Square, as they called it.

"And the lady was his companion:
Souple Corrigan.

"So anyway they were executed anyway and Souple Corrigan made his way to America."

"Corrigan was the only survivor of the gang, and there was either five or six in it.

"And what they spent their time at before they were catched was:

"They robbed rich men
  and they gave the money to poor men
    widow women,
    and orphans;
  and people like that, that was in poverty.

"And only for this incident,
 at this place,
  and it's supposed to be *Lisgoole*,
   they'd have got away thattime,
 only for the fellow insultin this *girl*,
 that this leader was givin him a chastisin
  for his rudeness and *badness*
  and all to this girl.

"And the forces arrived.

"And Corrigan made out and jumped the river
  and got away.

"And the rest of them was brought to Enniskillen."

PETER FLANAGAN

"His name in Irish, he was titled as Proinsias Dhu.

"That was the Irish style; it was Black Francis, he was Francis Corrigan in the English language.

"And he was known as a highwayman. In those days there was men and he was one of those highwaymen. His policy was: to rob the rich and serve the poor—give to the poor.

"And Lisgoole Abbey was started be monks, I understand, religious men, and he went this night and he robbed, he took a certain amount of stuff out of it in gold and silver.

"And the monks communicated with the military; in those days they were known as militiamen. The headman of them came out gallopin—it was all horse regiment thattime— and he came gallopin out.

"And Francis was goin toward Enniskillen, and he turned back.

"And they pursued after him: he's runnin and runnin from nearly Enniskillen on to Sillees River.

"And there was no bridge.

"And he leapt the twenty-foot river across.

"And says the headman of the regiment, he says:

"Corrigan, he says, that's a good jump.

"He says: the divil thank ye, he says,
    I had a long race for it ◊.

"So the chase continued.

"The headman of the army got across on a ford above
        and chased him on.

"And he came on
        as far as Derryhowlaght.

"And they were right on his heels there.

"And he took into the right there.

"And they went in after him
        on up towards a hill they call Druminiskill.

"And he was goin down the hill,

"And the horsemen was right on top of Derryhowlaght Hill;

        he threw the whole hoard of stuff into a hole.

"And he says, some man, he says, or woman, he says, will be rich some day.

"So it never was discovered from that day to this."

Mackan Fight   HUGH NOLAN

"Well, that was a fight, unfortunately, like many other fights that took place in this country. It was between Catholics and Protestants.

"Well, the Twelfth of July, do ye see, they do celebrate the victory at the Boyne in this country, the Ulster Protestants; they're known as the Ulster Orangemen.

"Well, this was on the thirteenth of July.

"And they started a parade from about Bellanaleck.

"And they paraded on up the road, and they were usin terrible
                    ah, terrible language towards the Catholics
                            as they went along.

"And they didn't spare their own side either, any of them that they didn't like. Because there was an old man tellin me that where Peter Monaghan lives now (you know that house there where you turn for Enniskillen) there was a Protestant man lived in that house.

"And he had a sow with a litter of pigs.

"And in them days, a sow, when she'd be goin to pig, would be brought into the *house*.

"And she'd be let have her pigs in the corner there.

"And they'd be kept in the house for about a week before they'd be put to some outhouse.

"And a couple of times a day, the sow used to go out, do you know, and come back *in* again.

"Well this parade was comin along.

"And this poor old man,
            and his wife,
                    their sow went out.

"And of course with the noise of these fellows comin along,

        didn't they forget about the sow.

"And there was one fellow,

        and he was walkin in front

        and he had a rifle.

"There was no rifles in them days; they weren't styled rifles, they were styled carbines.

"And there was a bayonet on the top of it.

"And the sow was on the road.

"On this side, if you remark it, there's a drinkin pool there, just at the foot of that brae, facin Crozier's gate.

"The sow was nosin about.

"And damn it, he run to the sow and he put the bayonet through her.

"Killed the sow on the poor old fellow.

"But they went on anyway.

"And the people away up the country, do ye see, heard the noise of them comin.

"And in them days, the Catholics, do ye see, they daren't have arms, but they did have weapons that they called pikes. The blacksmiths used to make them; ah, there was a lad and it was the shape of a fishin hook, do ye know; it was a blade, do ye see, kind of turned. And ye could run forward to a man and just give him the jab of it, do ye know.

"So anyway, the people all up the country, up be Mackan and round be Montiagh there,

        they all turned out with pikes

        for to meet these boys

        that was threatenin—

"Oh, they were threatenin to do everything that was rotten

on the Catholics
when they'd be comin back.
"So the two forces met, at a place they call Hannah's Cross. It's at the foot of Mackan Brae. Hannah's Cross it used to be called in days gone by. There was an old lady lived convenient to it; she was a Hannah Montgomery, and then this cross took its name from her.
"So the fight started *there*.
"And the Orangemen lost.
"The pikemen came in under them and they
    stabbed
       and whaled
          and finally the Orangemen retreated
            on down the road.
"And some of these wounded fell here and there
    along the road
       and others of them got dragged away.
"But anyway this man that killed this man's sow at Peter Monaghan's there, he got home.
"And I'll tell you where he lived.
"You know where John Moore lives there, in Rossawalla; it's the next house to Peter Monaghan's; when you're goin to Enniskillen it's on the same side of the road.
"Aye. Well, there's a farm up there. Peter Monaghan has it now. And there was several people livin on it, do ye know. It was in small wee lots at that time.
"Well, this man lived up there.
"He was the name of Scarlett.
"Well.
"He was brought home anyway.
"And the mother had a feed of sowens. That used to be a great luxury in Ireland in them days. It was what we'd call oaten gruel *now*, do ye know—oaten meal, boiled, not thick-

ened, but a nice drinkin, warm, do ye know, and there used to be sugar put on it—oh, it used to be great.

"So anyway, he took some of the sowens.

"And, savin your presence, I heared an old man sayin the sowens came out through the wounds.

"So it was wonderful direct punishment for what he done on the man goin up the road.

"So anyway there was a whole lot of Catholic fellows was arrested,

> and they were tried
> and they were sentenced to be *hanged*
> in Enniskillen.

"There was a jail in Enniskillen at that time, where the technical college is today. That was a jail in them days.

"So anyway, there was a petition sent to the Lord Lieutenant,

> and they were granted a reprieve:
> *transportation* for life,
> *six or seven* fellows.

"So there was one man was hanged afore the messenger *landed*

> from *Dublin*
> with the petition.

"So that's as far as I can give the details of the battle."

MICHAEL BOYLE

"Well, that was a religious fight.

"And, do ye see, at that time the men that professed the Protestant faith, do ye see, *they were in control.*

"See, the Catholic people had no life atall—just *they were slaves, they were serfs,* do ye see.

"Do ye see: there was no life for them, they had no livin. They were even apprehended and molested goin to their place of worship on Sunday.

"So anyhow, the Twelfth of July was a great day of celebrations, do ye see, for the Protestants and the *Orangemen* as they are known as. It was a great day of celebrations, do ye see.

"And they were celebratin—wherever they celebrated the Twelfth, I don't know, somewhere anyways, at some meetin.

"But the next day
    they assembled.

"And there was some trouble up at a place at Derrylin they call Mullineny. There was some trouble up there, another religious fight.

"But it twasn't as serious as the Mackan Fight turned out to be. I don't know whether there was any life lost in it or what now, but the word came down to these Orangemen in Ballymenone.

"There was alot of Orangemen in Ballymenone, do ye see—
    very terribly Protestant populated.

"And there was word came down, it was passed down to them, to go up to assist their brethren in Derrylin at Mullineny.

"So they set out on horseback anyway, a good many of them (they were nearly all on horseback), for to go to Mullineny and assist their brethren up *there*.

"So when they were goin over Mackan Hill,
    when they had came as far as Mackan Hill,
    they said that when they'd be comin back,
    that they wouldn't leave a Catholic house,
      but they'd burn it to the ground.

"So anyway, the boys didn't let them get any further.

"They got out.

"And the Orangemen was all armed with *guns*. The weapon at the time was an ould *gun* they called the musket.

"She fired a *ball*—oh, *deadly*, a deadly weapon.

"But she wasn't modern like the present-day gun; she was loaded at the muzzle, do ye see. She wasn't a needle gun, a breech-loadin gun; she was loaded at the muzzle. There was a handful of powder brought down the muzzle of her and a lump of paper put down after that, and twas rammed down with a *ramrod*. And then this ball was put in. Oh, I saw the ould balls; I seen a few that was kept for a souvenir. It was dropped in then, and another lump of paper put down, and rammed tight to keep it in its place, and then there was what they called a nipple. She was a wee lad about that length, do ye see, and the powder was packed into that. And when they were loadin, it was hit be the hand and the powder went into the nipple and there was what was called a cap put on the nipple, some kind of wee explosive cap, and then, do ye see, the hammer—when you pulled the trigger, the hammer fell on this cap and it exploded and put off the powder in the bore.

"Of course if that ball struck a man, it would go through him.

"It was death.

"But then, do ye see, you had to load again, and you had to load again.

"It was slow.

"But then it was the method used, do ye see, and them that was shootin against them had to do the same, do ye see.

"Well, these Orangemen were all armed with muskets, do ye see.

"Some of them had bayonets on them,
>> well prepared,
>> for the fight.

"But the poor Catholics, do ye see, had nothin, only pitchforks, pitchforks and every kind of weapons they could get their hands on.

"They sallied out
>> and attacked the boys.

"So faith, the boys didn't wait too much till they took to their heels,
>> and they run
>> for all they were worth.

"And the Catholics followed them
>> and prodded away at them,
>> and knocked them down on the roads,
>> and everything.

"But there was none of them killed outright,
> just that the chase went on,
> and there was a fellow,
> they called him Owney the Dummy,
> and he was workin at hay,
>> with a Protestant farmer
>> in a townland they called Clinulsen,
> and he heard the hullaloo,
> and he knew it was a fight,
> and he started away out of the hayfield,
> and he brought the pitchfork with him,
> and any man he got lyin on the road,
>> he killed him *out*.

"There were three Orangemen killed in the fight anyway.

"One of them was the name of Mealey. He lived in a place there on the Back Road; he's a man the name of Foster lives in it now. He's a Jim Foster.

"Well then, there was another man the name of Robinson and he lived in a townland they called Gortdonaghy.

"Well this Robinson lived *there*
and he was *killed*.

"And there was another man named Scarlett and he lived
in the townland of Gortdonaghy and he was killed also.

"There was three of them killed.

"But at any rate, that ended the fight;
they didn't burn the houses on Mackan Hill;
they run by them in the *slip*.

"They forgot all about it.

"But at any rate, of course, the Catholics was all arrested.

"I forget now the number of fellows that was arrested
and lodged in Enniskillen Gaol, but there was a trial before
the assizes, do ye see.

"The fight took place on the thirteenth of July, the day
after the Twelfth.

"And there was a wholesale arrest, do ye see, connected
with the fight, and a good many of them was sentenced to be
hanged. At the assizes in Enniskillen. They were sentenced to
be hanged.

"So there was a priest, he was a Father Ned McHugh, he
was a parish priest in Knockninny.

"And he rode a horse to Dublin
to petition to the Lord Lieutenant of the time,
the English Lord Lieutenant,
to *reprieve* these men.

"There was a whole lot of them wasn't guilty.

"They were proved guilty, but they weren't guilty; do ye
see: proved guilty on perjured evidence.

"So he rode a horse to Dublin.

"And he got the reprieve,
he got the reprieve,

the Lord Lieutenant reprieved them right enough.
"And Father Ned McHugh was comin with the reprieve.
"And it twas the day that was fixed for the execution.
"And he was *comin in the Dublin Road*.
"And he was *wavin it in his hand*,
    the way that *it twould be seen*.
"But *still they wouldn't wait*.
"*They hanged one man*.
"They hanged one man, his name was MacManus.
"He was Ignatius MacManus, he was from a townland they call Corcnacrea—Corcnacrea, it's in the Montiagh District; Corcnacrea, Mackan Post Office.
"Yes, he was hanged.
"They hanged him anyway, but then the priest was in. I don't know how many there was more, six or seven more, and the priest had came and they couldn't hang them.
"They couldn't hang them, but they transported them. They transported away to Van Dieman's Land; that is what is known as Australia at the present time. They were transported there.
"And after some few years in transportation,
    they were released,
    and they got farms,
    big wild Australian farms,
    and *they done the best*.
"*They done the best*.
"*They done the best*.
"They got on the best, better than what they would've done in this country, in Ireland at the time.
"So, you see, of course they communicated on with relatives for a long time.
"But then of course they've all died out now, do ye see.

"That fight took place in eighteen hundred and twenty-nine, do ye see, eighteen hundred and twenty-nine.

"But there is still a distant relation of Ignatius Mac-Manus, and he has a public house in Enniskillen. He owns a big bar there in Enniskillen, they call it the Central Bar. He's a stout strong block of a young red-haired fellow, a nice fellow when you come to chat with him. He's a distant relation of Ignatius MacManus.

"Aye, and he has an uncle livin there yet; he has an uncle livin up there yet. He is a Eugene MacManus, in the townland of Corcnacrea, all right. He's livin there with a family. And the two of them is distant relations of the man that was hanged for his part in the Mackan Fight: Ignatius MacManus.

"Ignatius MacManus had a son and I heard a story told about that too. He had a son that was watchin the execution, and he was only a small, very small wee fellow.

"And he never grew.

"He never grew any more.

"He was known as the Wee Man, as the Small Man for ever after—or the Wee Man as the ould people said.

"He was known as the Wee Man for ever after.

"He never grew after seein his father a-hangin."

"Well, we'll get back to Mackan Fight.

"There was a song on that. I know a verse of Mackan Fight.

"I heard it.

Twas on the thirteenth of July,
in the year of twenty-nine,
bein the time of these bloody No Surrenders.

"You see, No Surrender was the slogan of the Orangemen.

61

They were cheerin loud and shrill,
  till they came to Mackan Hill,
    for the face of a papish pretender.
Our gallant sons of fame,
  prefeciously they came,
    to confront these bloody tigers in battle.
And with our pitchforks made of steel,
  we forced them for to yield,
    though their bullets like hail did rattle.
Through malice and through spleen,
  they swore in nineteen,
    and all our loving brethren did suffer.
The first of our bleeding swains
  to fall from Montiagh plains
    was the gallant Ignatius MacManus,
Who with faith and courage bold,
  like a martyr he died on the gallows.
Where his innocent blood did fall
  it stained the flags and walls.
They scrubbed but all in vain,
  they never got it clean
    it remains there, a token of vengeance.

"That's some of it anyway."

HUGH PATRICK OWENS

"There was a fight at Mackan.

"It was a faction fight, what they call a faction fight. It was between Protestants and Catholics, you see.

"Well, they fought with billhooks and with scythes. There wasn't any guns. They had no guns.

"And a young priest was lookin out his window on Derryhowlaght. He was home, do ye see, and he was lookin out at the fight.

"And his mother says to him,
    the Catholics were losin and she says to him:
"For God's sake, Son, can you do nothin?
"He says, I was waitin for you to ask, he says.
"And he went into the Room, and he started prayin, and from that time on, the Catholics started winnin.
"And not another one was killed.
"Now, my father made a song on it. He made a song on that fight."

"Poetry makin was as easy as walkin for me father. He was well-educated. He'd sit in the corner there, makin them up.
"He could compose poems the best. Ah, he made a hat of them."

THOMAS OWENS

A Tourist-Visit-to Arney and Macken

To Arney a Tourist did find his way;
    he came along to pass the day.
At the Points he alighted and made for Cassidy's Store
    and his well stocked Bar that stands next-door.
He praised Jim's Biscuits, they were a treat,
    washed down by good Old Whiskey neat.
Soda water, stout, or wine,
    Jim Cassidy's Drinks are all genuine.
In a splendid Car Jim drove him round,
    as to his charges, no fault he found.
He expressed a wish to see Macken Hill;
    Jim drove him round with his good will.

He was told the story of the true men bold
      and heard the tale that was oft times told:
How the men of Macken the Yeomen defied,
      how they fought and conquered and on the Scaffold died.
The Yeos were all armed with baynot and Gun,
      from they Scythe blades and pitchforks they cut and run.
The Tourist back to Arney came,
      tired and thirsty but he was game.
He was greately pleased with his day out,
      and refreshed himself with boiled stout.
He put up a drink for those stand in round,
      and left for Enniskillen safe and sound.
His praise of Arney seemed sincere,
      for the Heros of Mackin he raised a cheer.

Note:

The times are changed for the better too,
We are no longer trampled by the Tyrant crew.
We can hold up our heads and hold them high
And will hold them higher in the near bye and bye.

The Tossing of the Chapel at Swanlinbar

PETER FLANAGAN

"The landlord gave an order that the place of worship, the chapel in Swanlinbar, had to be tossed.

"I don't know what year it twas. I think after Mackan Fight. It might be in eighteen and sixty or sixty-five. Mackan Fight was in twenty-nine, eighteen and twenty-nine. I think it twas in the late eighteen-hundreds anyway.

"He gave an order:
      the Swad Chapel had to be taken down,

64

and it had to be drawn away to build some castle.

"I didn't hear really what the stones or the buildin was goin to be converted into.

"But anyway, of course, the Catholics all opposed it.

"Why not?

"There and then.

"As the Protestants would, I suppose, if there was a church a-tossin.

"So them all assembled from all parts of Fermanagh, Cavan, Leitrim. They assembled all; it was the biggest gatherin ever there was.

"The Yeomen or the British army was goin to protect the men that was goin to take the chapel down.

"And they stayed about Swad for about a week. There was fifty or twenty thousand,
                    all prepared to fight.

"So the landlord reversed his decision about it. He said he'd call it off.

"There were troops comin from Enniskillen. Of course there was garrisons of troops here and there in Ireland, you know.

"And they were comin from all airts, so he gave the order that he'd extend the time to see and consider whether he'd toss it or not.

"So *nothin*, nothin happened, nothin ensued or nothin happened, and it was never tossed from that day till this."

JAMES OWENS

"And then at Florencecourt one time and they were goin to toss Swanlinbar Chapel.

"And there was a man there the name of Lord *Cole*.

"He lived up there where you see the mountains,
  he was goin to lead them,
    this mornin,
      to toss the chapel.
"And he wasn't turnin up, and they went to call him,
  and he was dead in bed.
"He was dead: he was black as your shoe.
"Do ye see now: the Almighty wasn't in favor of it.

"There is a monument there in Enniskillen yet, you know, Lord Cole's monument, out at the far end. That's the man was goin to toss the chapel.

"The IRA, they were goin to blow that up, and they were *caught*.

"Oh aye, they were caught. Some of the workmen left the gate open and they were *caught*. O Lord bless us, that would have been a powerful explosion: the *height* of it, do ye see. It would have done harm.

"It would have done harm to innocent people, do ye see. All them bricks and mortar and the *height* of that. Look at the length it was goin to go.

"It might have done harm surely.

"And there was a song about the Swad Chapel too.

"A cousin of mine, Missus Cox, and many a night she sang that song for us. And that was their favorite song. He'd come in from the pub and he'd have a few in, and it was the Swanlinbar Chapel Song he'd want to hear.

"I don't know now who made it, but I just forget the words of it at the present time.

"Och, longgo, you know, the ould people here used to tell lots of Irish history, but you weren't interested in it when you were young. When you were young you weren't interested. No, no.

"It was only afterwards that you just might mind some of the things that you heard about it."

The Swad Chapel Song
OWNEY MCBRIEN

You gentle muses
    pray excuse me
    for my intrusion on learning's wing.
And inspire my genius
    you bards and sages;
    my country's praises I mean to sing.
Tradition teaches
    without consultation,
    and blessed Patrick was first and all,
To Pope Celestine,
    and prune our vineyard,
    called Inisillgie or the Virgin Shore.

Ah, like Saint Peter,
    when his Master told him
    to feed his lambs and these flocks to keep,
He arranged the deserts
    the hills and mountains
    and plowed the ocean for the straying sheep.
He consecrated
    three hundred bishops,
    drove the snakes and serpents from our sainted isle,
And he told his people
    their church would suffer
    most persecution till the end of time.

It came to pass
    as the Saint predicted,
    for Satan's powers, as we are told,
They are now as strong as when
    he tempted Judas
    to sell our Savior for the love of gold.

The fallen angels,
    as yet impatient,
       they drove from heaven for creatin wars,
Has as lately tempted
    that ugly bailiff
       to seizin the temple in Swanlinbar.

Oh, had you been there
    on that Friday mornin,
       the twelfth of August or the night before,
When old Grania's sons
    they were well alarumed
       from Lisnaskea unto Ballinamore.
My boys prepare in
    a moment's warning
       ye shall be guided by the morning star.
For now is the time
    to repulse the tyrant
       and save our chapel in Swanlinbar.

From Leitrim mountains
    they came uncounted,
       from Cavan hills and Fermanagh gay,
Sayin, Where is the offspring
    of Martin Luther
       that dare opposes our church today?
Our valiant heroes
    from famed Drum Reilly,
       Drumlane, Knockninny, and Templeport,
And the warlike chieftain
    from Aughnacashelem,
       the Leitrim pikemen he led to sport.

As those Milesians
    they were all assembled
    in rank and order, in sept and clan,
Sure, I heard one chieftain
    say to another,
    Where are our brothers from unfaithful land?
Oh, Montiagh brave,
    have you been divided?
    You once won laurels, but now called slaves.
For your sons of order
    on the hills of Mackan
    would lose their lives or their chapel save.

My stupid brain
    cannot count the numbers,
    one hundred thousand exceeding far;
All payin homage
    to the star of Europe
    that saintly curate in Swanlinbar.

I'll lay down my pen now
    as the case is settled;
    come fill your glasses with rum and gin.
We will drink a health
    unto friend Montgomery
    to noble Maguire and Bennison.
I'll lay down my claim
    to the men of honor
    that ne'er was guilty of crime or wrong,
And the Swanlinbar boys
    cannot be forgotten;
    it's noble to call them old Grania's sons.

The Band JOSEPH FLANAGAN

"They had big flutes, wee flutes, and piccolos. They had the big drum and the wee drum. They were great bands, too, great.

"Oh man, you wouldn't be tired listenin to them. The Wearin of the Green. Old Folks at Home. The Harp Without the Crown. O'Donnell Abu. Napoleon's March. Oh man, they could play.

"But this old Troubles ruined that. Bigotry. It takes unity and peace in a country to do that. If a Catholic band went out now, they'd have to get a permit. And that left the people careless. They had no heart for goin out, you know. And now, surely, with the Trouble, it's worse.

"The old generation had a better interest in a band, you know; the young don't take an interest. And it's a bad thing in a way because a good band in a country is a great thing.

"If a good day comes on, boys-a-dear, it's a great thing to have a band turn out."

MICHAEL BOYLE

"Well this Old Ballymenone Band, do ye see, it was a good big band, quite a good flute band, do ye see.

"But then it lay in abeyance for a few years, do ye see. Some fellows left the country and the band lay up for a few years and no one was interested in it; the instruments were there, good instruments. And they were housed in a house down the road there—you might remark it, it's between Bellanaleck and Rossdoney. They're oil suppliers; a family of Moores lives in it; just on the roadside you see the oil tanks there and everything, oil storage tanks. Well, the band was there. It twas a family the name of Dugans were livin in it thattime. And that's where the instruments were, do ye see.

"And there was a big Sinn Fein meetin comin off in Enniskillen. It twas in nineteen hundred and seventeen. That was the year after the Rebellion, do ye see, in Easter Week.

"And our country, the Rossdoney end of Ballymenone, it was aligned, do ye see, with the rebels. It was all a rebel area. They were all Sinn Feiners.

"But the other end, the Back Road end, do ye see, they were all the opposite; they were opposed to the *whole* thing, do ye see.

"And the Rossdoney boys took a notion they'd get the band

        rigged up

          and bring it to this meetin in Enniskillen.

"And didn't they ask some of the Back Road boys would they come with them, do ye see, and form the band up again.

"And wouldn't they give in to go.

"But what did they do?

"They gathered up one evenin, ten or eleven of them, and they came up and they took the instruments out of Dugan's without notifyin anyone in *Rossdoney*, do ye see, any of the *Rossdoney* boys.

"And they went in and they asked the man of the house, Dugan, about the instruments, and, ah, they said they were goin to take them out for a tune, that they were long enough lyin there.

"And, damn it, he handed them out the instruments, do ye see,

        and there was no Rossdoney men.

"And as soon as he done that, he regretted it.

"He says, There's something wrong, he says, I don't see any of the Rossdoney men here, and they *should* be here.

"But the instruments was gone,
    and that was that,
        and away they went;
            the Back Road men took them, do ye see.

"They brought them away to the Back Road.

"So then of course the Rossdoney men heard it the next day, they were furious, do ye see, but there was no way of gettin them back. There was no good in goin for them, for they wouldn't give them to them, do ye see.

"So damn it anyway, they done a foolish thing of course—puttin the country to alot of expense—put themselves, Rossdoney, to alot of expense. They went away and they took legal proceedins against them, do ye see, for the recovery of the instruments.

"But it twas tried here in Enniskillen before the County Court judge. He dismissed the case.

"He dismissed it, do ye see, he wouldn't give judgment for Rossdoney.

"So then that was that.

"They appealed the case before the judge of assizes.

"And they were beaten again.

"And that heaped on extra costs.

"The Rossdoney men was payin the cost for years and years, do ye see, and had no instruments.

"But then there was an ould set of instruments lyin on, do ye see, that, well they thought was wore out, do ye see; they had got new ones. And didn't they rig up the old instruments and started a second band in Rossdoney, with the result that there was *two bands* goin for a few years.

"But then this Trouble came along.

"Nineteen and twenty:
    nineteen and twenty,
    the shootin and the trouble here, do ye see,

and both bands went into abeyance anyway.

"But anyway what happened the followin years, do ye
see, the Republican IRA at a time,
    they gathered up one night,
    and they went down to the Back Road.

"They weren't admitted, do ye see, but they had to break
in the doors.

"They broke in the two doors ◊ and they cleaned the
whole instruments out ◊.

"They cleared the whole damned instruments away.

"And I don't know what they done with them,
    destroyed them I suppose.

"They cleared them away anyway ◊.

"And that ended the Ballymenone Band."

"Well, do ye see, the Back Road men, they were called
Molly Maguires. Hibernians, they were called, but they were
originally the ould Molly Maguires, do ye see.

"They belonged to the ould Irish party, do ye see. The
ould Irish party was led be John Redmond, do ye see. Then
they belonged to it. And, do ye see, the Rossdoney ones
joined up with the new Sinn Fein party. Aye.

"So that's how the split came in the Ballymenone Band.

"Aw, it *ruined our country*.

"It ruined that whole District for years and years.

"Do ye see, it was a terrible *spite*.

"Oh, it ruined it for years and years.

"And the first thing that united it was the football team,
    the Bellanaleck football team.

"See, there was a football team away back before my day,
but then of course the fellows that played in it, they got old
and some of them emigrated, do ye see, and with the result
that the team died out for years and years.

"So a lock of us young fellows got our heads together and we took a notion we'd start *another* team.

"*So we did.*

"And took in fellows from both ends, do ye see, from the Rossdoney end and the Back Road end and all, and we got up a great football team.

"Well then the people all got out to the football matches, with the result that it was the first thing here *healed up that split.*

"*And it did.*

"And the football team's goin to the present day:

a good wee team yet,
the Bellanaleck Art MacMurroughs they're called.

"The first team that ever was formed in Ballymenone was called the Art MacMurroughs.

"And the man that formed it, that was the means of it bein formed, was the teacher that taught me and taught all the young fellows, Richard Corrigan. He was the first man to start football, the Gaelic games, in Ballymenone.

"Aye, indeed.

"And it was it brought the two sides together. It was ridiculous the way they were carryin on.

"Course, I suppose the anger was about the instruments bein taken and everything and,

why,
there'd be two rival crowds
at the chapel gate,
one standin here,
and one standin there,
and them jeerin at other, you see.

"It was ridiculous.

"And then to make things worse, do ye see, it was a big Protestant community, and the Protestant population was laughin at them, was just *laughin* at them.

"Well, that was the first thing healed the split anyway that was caused by the band."

"You know that old poet, Hugh McGiveney, he made a poem on it, and a song on the band. It had an air; there was an air of its own put to it. And the poem run:

Johnny dear and did you hear
    the news that's goin around:
Our band it has been stolen
    away from holy Sinn Fein ground.
It was stolen by John Redmond's men,
    a pack that's low and mean,
And the reason that they took it
    was to murder poor Sinn Fein.

They dragged it off to prison,
But martyrs don't complain.
They forcibly threatened, tortured it,
And its only crime Sinn Fein.
But we will liberate it,
And it will sound again,
And strike a blow for Ireland's rights,
    and its own beloved Sinn Fein ◇.

Ah now, Paddy, let me tell ye,
The meanest thing that crawls,
Who apes to be an Irishman,
    brought up in a Saxon hall,
He stole away I. M. Sullivan's band,
Twas well worthy of its name.
But we will liberate it,
And it will sound again,
To strike a blow for Ireland's rights,
    and its own beloved Sinn Fein.

We have Mackan and ould Montiagh,
And faithful Inishmore,
The gallant Larkin and O'Brien,
They were loyal to the core.
We have Rossdoney and Drumbargy,
Rossawalla and Drumane,
Who swear they'll die or conquer
To rescue our band
    and restore it to Sinn Fein.

"Now wait'll I see now. There's another verse:

So now me boys take warnin:
When fillin up your ranks,
Don't get beat to your bandroom
By red slaves or cranks;
Don't put your trust in Redmond,
William Trimble or the D.I.,
And when life remains all in your veins,
Let Sinn Fein be your cry.

"That's the song.
"That was made be Hughie McGiveney of Rossdoney."

The Brookeborough Raid   ELLEN CUTLER

"Och, it's sad seein wee childer out throwin rocks. They don't know any better. Their parents teach them.

"And it's the very same with the leaders. They send poor stupid lads out to do the work. Like that Brookeborough Raid.

"There was a lad the name of O'Hanlon. He was wounded. And some of his men took and left him in an old house or a byre. And he told alot of news when he was found. Gave them information about his side, you see. And then he asked for first aid and one of the boys of our side says, This is first aid enough for you, and hit him with the butt of a rifle.

"Now wasn't that terrible?

"And this other boy South, that was with them, he said that they would be killed if they had come back without carryin out their orders.

"And wasn't *that* terrible? Ah now.

"This South was a spy. He came all through the country into houses, sellin Old Moore's Almanac and old books and clothes and brushes. And many people seen him.

"A Sheridan boy over be Florencecourt put up a ladder to his hay, and went up it, and South jumped out, jumped off from the top of it. He recognized him. I heard him talkin about it down here. So I did.

"I never seen him, but I heard about it."

Sean South
GABRIEL COYLE

It was on a dreary New Years' Eve as the shades of night fell down,
A lorry load of volunteers approached a border town;
There was men from Dublin and from Cork, Fermanagh, and Tyrone.
But the leader was Limerick man, Sean South of Garryowen.

And as they marched along the street up to the barracks door,
The sergeant spied their daring plan, he spied them through the door.
Aye, with Sten guns, aye and from rifles too, a hail of death did fall.
And when that awful night had passed, two men lay cold as stone.
There was one from near the border and one from Garryowen.

No more they will hear the sea gulls' cry o'er the murmuring Shannon
    tide,
For they fell beneath that northern sky, brave Hanlon by his side.
They have gone to join that gallant band of Plunkett, Pearse, and Tone.
Another martyr for old Ireland, Sean South of Garryowen.

The Flag That Floats Above Us   PETER FLANAGAN

The slave may bend in abject fear,
And he may hug the chains that bind him,
And the coward may run his base career,
No flag of freedom find him.
But while above us floats the flag,
Of green and orange blended,
No tyrant, nor no knave, its folds shall drag
While our stout arms defend it.

We ask for not but what's our own
Of friend nor foreign foeman.
We are one in love and blood and bone
We yield nor we bend to no man.
We fight the fight our fathers fought
Beneath that same old standard,
And they nobly died, as brave men ought,
While leading freedom's vanguard.

Gaze on that standard as it flies,
By true man's hand supported,
A prouder yet neath heaven's skies,
A fairer never floated.
It waved o'er O'Brien and O'Neill,
O'er Sarsfield, Tone, and Emmet.

WAR

It oft has braved the foeman's steel
And foemen's blood begem it.

No hireling, servile slaves are we
To bend with mock submission
To the alien's grinding, tyrant he,
And despot's fierce ambition.
But for our own, our suffering land,
Ten thousand hearts are ready,
For to strike a blow against alien wrong,
Calm, patient, firm, and steady.

And we'll shout it out to foe or friend,
To those who hate or love us,
While life remains we will defend
The flag that floats above us.

THE LAND

The Croziers' home. View west from the Derrylin Road that cuts through the community, leading to Mackan.

Days of the Landlords   HUGH PATRICK OWENS

"The land through here was what they called the School Lands. It run from Lough Erne to Binn Mountain. And the agent was a man the name of Bennison; he collected the money at Ballyconnell, up in County Cavan.

"Do ye see: the land was all owned by landlords.

"See, they all had big estates for themselves. They had big crops. And they'd come by and if you wanted to save your wee harvest, they could order you away to theirs, leavin yours to rot. That's the way it went on for hundreds of years.

"At that time, you could make no will. When you died your family could be out on the road in a week.

"And the landlords are bound to rackrent.

"So, they fought the landlords for ages. They formed up the Land League and they called big meetins. And they marched here and there and agitated, the same as they are doin at the present time, to show the government they were all in favor of this thing. They had bands and banners and they made speeches.

"Now, that's the way they done it: they organized and held big meetins.

"And they got rid of the landlords. The government bought them out, you see, and gave you a tenant rate on the land. And then you'd pay rent to the government. And the government gave them a big reduction. The rent was half or less than half of what it was before. And they couldn't be evicted.

"You got a receivable order, do ye see, and you went to the bank in Enniskillen in May and November and you paid your half a year's rent.

"Before that you could be evicted any time. And they did it. They did it.

"And there was no reason to improve your property. You couldn't own it or sell it. You had no deed.

"It was the first great victory ever they got was to get rid of the landlords.

"Before that, the landlord came and if he seen a decent cake of bread on your table, you could be out on the road Monday mornin.

"Oh aye."

HUGH NOLAN

"There used to be old mansions, do ye know, that had decayed and that had fallen, and they were generally all built with stone. Well, them stones wouldn't want so much dressin. And then there was people had them old ruins on their land. And they could get a house built handy.

"I mind there was a mansion
        up in Drumbargy
                in days gone by.

"And it was a gentleman's residence. It was just beside John Carson's. I saw the ruins of it. Well, it wasn't standin when I seen it, but the stones it was built with was all there.

"And I mind John Carson's uncles, they got an office-house built out of the ruins of this. It was a whole stone *buildin*.

"It was just beside Missus Carson's. When you was goin forward to Missus Carson's *house*, this mansion was on your *right*, just where the plantation is *now*.

"I'll tell you who he was. He must have been a Frenchman.

"And I'll tell you what he was. He was a clergyman, a Church of Ireland clergyman. And he was what they called a middleman.

"After the Plantation of Ulster, the lands was given be the king to the gentry, to English and Scotch settlers.

"And they'd be what they called *landlords*.

"Well, some of them didn't come to Ireland atall to live. But these what they called the middlemen, *they* took the land from the landlords at a rent, do ye see. And then they set it then in small farms and in large farms to *tenants*, do ye see. That'd be the common people.

"Well, there was alot of them middlemen. They were livin here and there through the country. This man lived in Drumbargy. This man, he was LaDew. He was a William LaDew. That's a French name. Well then there was another of these middlemen and he lived in Tonyheig. He was the name of Acheson. And different other places there was men of that type.

"Well, this LaDew, he owned Drumbargy and Ross-doney, and whether he owned any more possessions else-where, I can't tell ye. But he had this taken from whoever the landlord was at that time. The landlord might have been in London or some other place. And he lived in this house, up on the top of the hill.

"So after some time, them men went out of existence, and the houses was unoccupied and finally they fell and *disappeared.*

"And the middlemen faded away and it was back in the landlords' hands again, and then there was *agents* appointed then for to collect the rents. And there was another position in connection with it: the bailia. There was a man that would be in every district that used to watch the tenants, do ye see, and not let them be abusin the land or doin any harm.

"The bailia—or bailiff—they weren't liked at all. They were hated; they were hated.

"He was under the agent. The agent was under the landlord, and the bailia was under the agent.

"I just don't know whether these type of men was on all the estates or not, but they were on the Schoolands anyway. Do ye see: after some time it was the Commissioners of Education bought this estate that Rossdoney's on, and Drumbargy, and it was known from that as the Schoolands.

"There has been changes all down the ages. And whoever that the landlord was that this LaDew had the land taken from, maybe his family became extinct, and that it was taken over be the Commissioners of Education.

"Well then, there was a man lived up at Ballyconnell. He was—aw, he was a gentleman. He was the agent. And then these other boys was a-*watchin* for him, and if you cut a tree or done anything like that, do ye see, it went to the agent and from him to the landlord and it could be the cause of you bein evicted. Aye.

"At one time there lived a bailiff in that house beside Andy Boyle's, the Keenans', and there was a bailiff there for a while.

"And there was a bailiff at a cross on the Swad Road.

"Do ye see, the course that this demesne took, it started here on the shores of Lough Erne, and it took a vein with it nearly up to Swanlinbar.

"Sometimes it was very narrow and sometimes it widened out, do ye see. It took a kind of a bend and Sessiagh and Derrychurra was a part of this estate. And how them two townlands got to be part of the Schoolands is what I don't know, for I never heard, nor—of course, I suppose, if I had been interested enough in it when the old people was all livin, they might have been able to give some explanation about it, but I came to the conclusion that it was a *purchase*, that the Commissioners of Education, *or* whoever owned the Schoolands before they got it, that them townlands was a purchase that they made.

"Well, then there was other demesnes then on both sides of it owned be landlords. The Schoolands would lie between Cole's demesne and Kinawley. Lord Enniskillen owned Clontymullan and on up towards the Hangin Rock; that was all Cole's demesne.

"And there was some of these demesnes and they were just owned be men that raised, well, be *good pull* and be industry that had got to be landowners, do ye see. But it was the Commissioners of Education that owned this at the time that the Land Acts came along that the landlords were all disqualified or paid off. The Agitation started and finally the government took the land over. And the people got what they called Tenant Right. They got to be owners of whatever land they possessed. They could sell it or keep it or will it or do what they liked.

"Well, there was some of them estates remained in the hands of the landlords for some time after the Agitation. And then they got what they called *bought out*—bought out be the government, do ye see.

"There had to be acts passed, do ye see, in Parliament, do ye see, for to take the land from these and compensate them, do ye see.

"So the government compensated these owners and then they fixed a rate then on the land for takin it away. So the people was payin that on till whatever the government had gave for the land. When they got it back, do ye see, the land was rent free.

"How that happened was: there started what they called the Land League in Ireland. And that was a movement against the landlords. Their points was that the rents was too *high* and that the conditions wasn't suitable to the people and so on. And that Agitation went on and went on and finally the government took it over and set it out.

"It was a campaign, do ye know, a campaign for to relieve the farmin class.

"It was considered a wonderful victory."

PETER FLANAGAN

"There were tenants that sided with the landlords. They weren't much liked in this country. Ah, they were not.

"They got backhand or castle money, as the word was.

"There was the Lord Lieutenant's office in Dublin at that time, and they would pay these people to follow the landlord. Then you and I, we would disagree, and there would rise anger between us and the tenants that got this backhand money.

"That's a trouble that is still with us at the present time. The rich men don't want to loss their good jobs, or their power, and they keep the poor class of people split apart and fightin.

"That's the way, now."

Mrs. Timoney's Remarkable Walk
MICHAEL BOYLE

"There was old men about, and the people didn't get information enough off them, do ye see. People could have learned far more of the olden days from the older people.

"Now, I remember an old woman in our country.

"She was the name of Timoney. She'd be some friend

88

of Jimmy, the present Jimmy Tumblety's. She lived where Tommy Love's livin; that's where she lived.

"And she had a wee farm. Her husband had it. Her husband died when she had three of a family, two girls and a boy.

"And her husband died when her family was small, do ye see.

"She had to go out the best she could. As well as doin the wee bit of housework, she had to go out to the field and labor with the spade, tryin to earn a little money, put in a crop to try to rear the wee family.

"And the rate of that land in Rossdoney had to be paid to a man, that Bennison, John Joe Bennison of Ballyconnell.

"You had to go beside Ballyconnell Town, and you had a big lot of hours to walk; there was no other way of goin thattime.

"She had the rate ready for to go to Bennison's this day,
    and she out to Bennison's
      and when she arrived at Bennison's,
        she was late.

"Her name was sent down to Enniskillen to the Crown Solicitor to serve her with the Provost; well then, he could bring her to court.

"The clerk at Bennison's office told her, says he:
"If you could get to Enniskillen
    before three o'clock the day
      you'd save the costs;
      they wouldn't put the costs on.

"So she set out from Ballyconnell,
    and she walked down to Enniskillen
    after walkin from Rossdoney to Ballyconnell.

"She set out and she walked from Ballyconnell to Enniskillen
    and she was there before three o'clock

and she saved the costs.

"And when she had it all paid, she had one shillin in her pocket.

"One shillin.

"And she bought a quarter stone of oatmeal,
	and a pound of sugar with the shillin.

"And she walked home to Rossdoney,
	and she made a noggin of what they call gruel.

"It's great stuff, gruel, a great reviver. It's made out of oatmeal. It twasn't made as thick as porridge; it's made nice and thin. It's the same as sowens, only it's tastier than sowens, and she sweetened it well with sugar.

"And she took a great feed of that and went to bed,
	and got up the next mornin
	and went out on a hill
		with the spade
		and dug lea
			the whole day
	after the whole walk.

"Didn't that old woman live to be ninety. I remember *her*. I *remember* her, and was talkin to her often.

"And she was only a small woman. I remember her. I think I can see her yet: she wore a wee white cap over her head always, and Irish lace trimmed round it, and tied with a nice wee bow here, and she wore what they call a shawl-handkerchief over her shoulders.

"She lived to be over ninety years of age. I remember the time she died. I was often talkin to her. She remembered the tail end of the Famine, the famine that was in Ireland in forty-six. She remembered that. Them times were terrible.

"Her father was a shoemaker, and I used to remember her sayin she'd have to go to Enniskillen a couple of times a week to buy leather for him and, well, stuff, nails and spriggs for the boots; for he was the shoemaker. They called him Mickey the Warrior. Mickey the Warrior was the name they had on him.

"And, aye, she used to say she saw people lyin along the road just exhausted with pure hunger. Aye. Oh, I remember her sayin she remembered the tail of the Famine.

"She was married to this man, Timoney. Her name was McGiveney. She was some friend of that Hugh McGiveney. She was."

HUGH NOLAN

"I seen that woman meself. I *knew* her.

"And the way the story went:

"The people had to go to Ballyconnell to pay their rate.

"And she was a poor widow-woman.

"And she had just the rate gathered up.

"And she had to go some business to Town, to Enniskillen first.

"So she came to Enniskillen here and she done whatever business she had to transact.

"And she got, I think,
         a bowl of soup.

"She couldn't afford to get any more because she'd have to break in the rate.

"And she started out of Enniskillen,
         and she walked to Ballyconnell,
              and walked back to Rossdoney again.

"It was a terror.

"Well that would be in the beginnin of the nineteenth century.

"Oh, I seen the woman. I seen the woman.

"At this time that she done this Remarkable Walk, her

91

husband was dead. And she had two little girls, and they were only *children*.

"Well, when I came to know her, she was livin with the son-in-law and a single daughter.

"It was in the house where Tommy Love lived."

The Famine   HUGH NOLAN

"You see:
"In days gone by,
　　　　but it's a very long time since,
　　　　　there was no such crop in Ireland as spuds.
"The spuds was imported.
"It was one of Queen Elizabeth's generals, at the time that they were a-conquerin Ireland. To the best of my opinion, it was. He brought the spuds, he brought the spuds to Ireland.

"And the first place they were grew, I think, was in County Cork.

"Well, before that, it was wheat, oats, and barley that was the crops that used to be put in. There might be vegetables too, but there was no such thing as spuds.

"So, these crops, they gave great employment. They were all put in with spades and loyas. And then there was a big job then
　　　　　at the cuttin of them
　　　　　and the gatherin of them
　　　　　and the lashin and the thrashin of them
　　　　　　and till they had it ready for the mills.
"Well then, there was a lot of mills in Ireland at that time.
"And they were all workin, with a fairly big staff.
"Well, there was no such thing as tea

in them days.

"*But,* if you were travelin *there,*
     there was what they called along the roadsides:
          there was *inns.*

"That was places where you could get a meal.

"Well there was at one time in Ireland that you could get a wonderful great meal of *milk,* and either wheaten bread or oaten bread. There used to be oaten bread made. There was irons for bakin in them days. The women used to wet the oatmeal and make it into the shape of a cake, do ye know.

"And these irons went round the fire.

"And this bread baked hard.

"And you wanted to have good teeth.

"But it was lovely with butter.

"Well, in them days you could get a wonderful great meal of sweet milk,
     either wheaten bread or oaten bread,
          well buttered,
               for tuppence,
                    if you were travelin.

"Well, the pretties was introduced. And it was discovered that one man could put in durin the spring as much spuds as would do his household till thattime twelvemonth. And if he had extras they could be give to cattle and pigs.

"Well, the *oat*—
     the *corncrop*—
     and the *wheatcrop,*
     and the *barley,*
          it died out.

"And it caused a wonderful lot of emigration. Because these men that was workin in these mills had to quit, do ye see, when there was nothin for them to do, do ye see. So these men had to emigrate to foreign countries.

"So then, the prettie crop, it got very common.

"And there was two famines.

"There's not so much talked about the first famine. The first famine, I think, was about the year of seventeen and forty. It was a failure in the potato crop. Because they were livin practically on the potatoes.

"There were some used to have a lock of oats. And they'd take their breakfast of porridge. And then they'd have the dinner of spuds. And then before they'd go to bed at night, they'd have another feed of spuds. And they had plenty of sweet milk of coorse then at the same time.

"But these two years, the potato crop was a total failure.

"And they had nothing to eat.

"And alot of them died.

"Well then in eighteen and forty-six then came the second part of the famine.

"And it was a *worse*—a worse famine. Because the population of Ireland had riz at that time to eight million.

"So.

"Aw, they died in scores.

"Britain was blamed.

"They had wheat and meal and other things that they could let out and didn't.

"So anyway, between *death and emigration*, when the Famine was over, it was down to about four million.

"So it has never riz since.

"So there was relief works was started here and there durin the time of the Famine. But then, do ye see, the men wasn't able to work because they had nothin to eat.

"So it was a terrible calamity.

"And the result of it is to be felt to this day.

"Emigration: any of them that was able to leave the country, they went out of it. And then emigration started wholesale. And as soon as young men grew up, they were away. That's how there's so many Irish in America. In Australia. These countries that took in emigrants."

Mr. McBrien   MICHAEL BOYLE

"There was a man named McBrien.

"He lived somewhere in Rossdoney, in the Point of Rossdoney as they call it.

"And he had a *wife*
>and five children,
>>five young children.

"And they hadn't a haet; there was no food,
>there was no food,
>>and they were in a starvin condition.

"And he said he'd *fish*;
>he'd try and fish in the Arney River,
>>that run along his land,
>>that was convenient to his land.

"He said he'd fish,
>try and fish to see would he get a few fish to eat
>>that'd keep them from dyin.

"So he did; he went out this day,
>and he caught seven fish.

"Well he went every day,
>well for a good many days.

"And he caught seven fish every day.

"And one of the children died anyway.

"And he caught six then.

"And he caught *six every day*.

"The number went down to six.

"Aye, I heard that too, about the time of the Famine. That

happened in Rossdoney, the townland of Rossdoney, along the Arney River there.

"Now that happened; it was told anyway.

"It came down from the Famine days."

Castle Garden   PETER FLANAGAN

Farewell my old acquaintance, my friends both one and all,
My lot is in America, to either rise or fall.
From my cabin I'm evicted and likewise compelled to go
From that lovely land called Erin where the green shamrocks grow.

Hurray my boys the sails is spread and the wind is blowing fair.
Full steam for Castle Garden, in a few days we'll be there.
For to seek for bread and labor as we are compelled to go
From that lovely land called Erin where the green shamrocks grow.

I owe the landlord two years' rent and I wished I owed him more.
One day a cowardly bailiff stuck a notice on my door.
My old and wearied mother, it grieved her heart full sore,
For to leave the house my father built, twas sixty years or more.

(Chorus of second stanza)

Farewell my old acquaintance, with whom I used to sport,
Where we'd sing and dance on a Sunday night where the girls used to resort.
For there's one I leave behind me, and she grieves my heart full sore,
For to leave her in old Ireland. Will I ever see her more?

Hurray my boys the sails are spread and the wind's yet blowing fair,
Full steam for Castle Garden, in a few days we'll be there.
For to seek for bread and labor as we are compelled to go
From that lovely land called Erin where the green shamrocks grow.

Skibbereen

JOHN O'PREY

Oh, it's father dear, I often hear you speak of Erin's isle,
Her lofty green, her valley scenes of mountains wide and high.
They say it is a lovely place wherein a prince might dwell.
Oh, why did you abandon it? The reason to me tell.

Oh, my son, I love my country with energy and pride.
Till a blight came over our crops, and our sheep and cattle died.
The rents and taxes were so high that them we could not redeem,
And them's the cruel reasons why we left old Skibbereen.

It's well I do remember that bleak December day.
When the landlord and the sheriff came to drive us all away.
They sent our roof on fire with their damning yellow spleen,
And when it fell the crash was heard all over Skibbereen.

When you were a boy of two years old and feeble was your frame,
We could not leave you with your friends, you bore your father's name.
We wrapped you up in our old frieze coat by the dead of a night unseen,
And we bid a sigh and said good-bye to dear old Skibbereen.

So it's well I do remember the year of forty-eight,
When we'd arise with Erin's boys to battle for the Fenian.
We were hunted as outlaws and traitors to the Queen,
And them's the best of reasons why we left old Skibbereen.

So it's father dear the day is near when vengeance loud will call,
When we will rise with Erin's boys, to rally one and all.
I'll be the man to lead the van beneath the flag of green.
Ah, it's right loud and high we'll raise the cry: Revenge for Skibbereen.

Lovely Erne's Shore

OWNEY MCBRIEN

When I was young and foolish, my age being twenty-four,
I left Lough Erne's lovely banks and to Boston I sailed o'er,
And there I met a lady gay of honor and renown,
And from her shores I asked the way to famous New York town.

What do you think young man, she says, along with me to stay,
And let us talk of Ireland and Lough Erne another day.
I have ranches down in Texas, I have horses by the score,
And I'll lead you down to the Rio Grande, it's far from Erne's shore.

Ah no, kind lady, pardon me, your wealth I do disdain.
I'll go with you some other day, your fond love to maintain,
For there is no night or lady bright is half so fair as you,
But Erin's dells, its braes and glens to leave them I would rue.

How could I leave Lough Erne's banks where my young Molly dwells?
Your castles and your mansions are to me like prison cells.
Were you ever on Lough Erne when the sun was setting low,
And the purple and the heather and the hills a fiery glow?

Your castles and your mansions are the best that e'er was owned,
Your steers and donkeys in the ring are the best in San Antone,
But I'd give them all had I my call and more I would bestow
For to feast my eyes on Ireland and lovely Erne's shore.

Ah, the fair of Enniskillen is the grandest fair of all,
For the colleens are the sweetest and the boys they are straight and tall.
So, I'll bid adieu to Texas too, for I'll see it never more,
For I'm going back to Ireland and lovely Erne's shore.

THE LAND

A Lovely Country HUGH NOLAN

"Well, there was a very comical man lived in this town-land, very witty, you know. And there has been people that moved away and then they came back.

"And funny enough: there was people that got dogs from other localities, and didn't the dogs go back to their own country.

"So. This comical man said, I don't know what there is in this country, he says, but it seems always the same to me: when people are taken away, they come back.

"Aye ◊.

"Well.

"And there was a man that lived at Mackan, and he lived there his whole life.

"He had never been out.

"And one sunny day, a neighbor came upon him.

"And he was just standin, lookin out on the fields just, and he says:

"It's a lovely country, he says, a lovely country altogether.

"He was like a visitor that had never been here, do ye see, never been here before,

and he *lived here his whole life*.

"Well, Ireland is lovely. And there'd be nobody leavin atall if there was a way to make a pound here, the same as what there is in America or Australia, or, nearer by, England or Scotland."

The Fermanagh Song
MARTIN CRUDDEN

Good people all, on you I call, and this song I will sing to you.
Twas written with a loving hand, each word is fond and true.
It's all about Fermanagh, and the first thing I will do
Is take you to the Hangin Rocks near the village of Belcoo.

There's lovely Devenish Island with its tower so tall and grand,
Its lovely lapping waters and its stretch of deep brown sand.
The lovely hills of Knockninny have a beauty rich and rare
Where as a child I roamed for miles without worry or without care.

When tourists visit our country, sure, the first place that they seek
Is our world famous pottery and its china that's unique.
For we that are familiar, sure, there's no need for to speak,
For when you mention pottery you can only mean Belleek.

Of all Fermanagh's beauty spots, I can only mention some,
And one of them must surely be the castle down at Crom.
There's lovely Enniskillen and likewise dear Lisnaskea,
And when you visit Fermanagh all these places you can see.

And if you come along with me, it is proudly we will march,
By the winding roads through Florencecourt to the lovely Marble Arch.
And it will be my pleasure for to show you all these and more
When you come to visit Fermanagh on Lough Erne's lovely shore.

THE PEOPLE

Hugh Nolan.

"Well then, in old times in this country—well, I didn't hear it told, but I seen it in print—in some houses, in the kitchen, they used to have the fire in the center of it.

"Well then, when the ceiliers would come in then, of a winter's night, they could all sit in a ring around the fire.

"They could play cards and them sittin at the fire. Tell stories and sing, and I suppose if they took a notion of dancin, there was room enough for them to dance around the fire, do ye see.

"I never seen it, nor I never heard any of the old people talkin about seein it, but they was in existence, especially with the poorer classes.

"Well, the poorer classes, do ye see, was always counted the jolliest.

"Well, you could associate more with them than with the Big Bucks in all ages, do ye see.

"Well, do ye see the way it is, the poorer and plainer people, they get made to this hardship. And it's their life. It's their life, do ye see.

"They get made to it.

"But of course at the present time, the younger generation now in this country wouldn't go in as much for *hardship* as what their ancestors. They wouldn't go in for the system of working that they had. Nor, they wouldn't have the same patience.

"They wouldn't have the same patience. If they can't get the job done quick, it's goin to be an encumbrance to them, do ye see.

"Well then, I suppose how that has come about: there has came through many types of machinery, that young men has got away from the old system of the spade and the scythe and the shearin hook and all these weapons that you lost plenty of sweat.

"When I first mind the harvest, the meadows were all mowed with scythes. In my early days, when I got out on the road, it was all scythes: three men, one after another, mowin away from mornin to night.

"Well then, the mowin machines came then and no one would go out with a scythe. A man would cut his hay and look at his neighbor and see that he could do in an hour what took him two days. And you couldn't get a man to do it.

"And I'll tell ye, longgo when the turf was a-cuttin—you see, there's very little turf now a-cuttin in the old way—well, there'd be men in the bog. And they'd be workin hard. And dinner time would come. And when dinner'd be over, maybe all that was in the bog workin, they'd gather together, and there'd be a smoke and a ceili and the wait of an hour before they'd resume again.

"And then there was another custom: if there was two men workin beside other they could chat from one job to the other and work away, do ye see. Aye.

"But, do ye see, that has all ceased now. Because when you're on a job, well, ye'll get so long of a break for lunch and the like of that, and when that's over maybe there'd never be a word spoke, do ye see, when they'd be takin their lunch."

"Sure, chattin as they used to call it, it has nearly went out of existence with television and radios and all these things. The people's continually listenin. They're not talkin atall. Continually listenin.

"They may have a few words with other. But they're listenin to something on the radio or on the television.

"Aye, indeed."

THE PEOPLE

ELLEN CUTLER

"The Lunnys are good neighbors. They're the best now.

"Tommy's mother often sent up a lump of butter, nice and sweet and good.

"And I seen John James, Tommy's brother, he's dead now, comin up the lane with a whole cart of pretties and puttin them in the shed at the back.

"For some reason, there was none here. The crop was bad. And they brought many's the prettie here for us.

"And you daren't offer them anything.

"Billy and Johnny gave them a big hedge for firin, and they never forgot.

"Tommy does come by and borrow the ladder to thatch his pecks of hay. And he always stops by to see is there any wee thing I need. Ah, they're the best.

"Tommy's father used to come to ceili with Billy. Billy had a pipe and they'd sit at the fire there, passin it back and forth."

ROSE MURPHY

"They had clay for brick. They had their own trees. They cut the trees and made their roof.

"They had their own thatch and thatched it. It didn't cost a thousand pounds either.

"They lived, didn't they? They lived."

HUGH NOLAN

"And in days gone by, they used to what was styled *swappin*.

"I went to *you*
        the *day*.

"And then I had something the morrow and you came to *me*.

"And then I went back to you then the next day and so on. That the work was got done. *Two* men's work would be goin on at a time.

"That was the way.

"And then there was the methal.

"It used to apply to where there'd be a man that wasn't in good form. Or that some one of his family was sick.

"And that he wasn't able to work himself, nor he wasn't able to get workin with the trouble that was in the house.

"Well then, on a certain day then, *all* the men of the locality would all turn out, and maybe they'd put in a whole field of spuds. Or put in a field of oats or *some* thing like that, do ye know.

"And if it was in the hay season, they done for a day, and if he had his hay raised up, it'd be all put up, do ye see. That was the way. *Groups* like that, that's what they were called: methals. The whole men in the locality went out for a day to one particular man, or to a widow-woman. Aye.

"It was a common thing to happen in this part of Fermanagh.

"I seen often nine and ten men in one field, workin for some man, as I was tellin you, that wasn't able for to do it himself. Or that there was some trouble about the house that he couldn't get it done."

THE PEOPLE

HUGH PATRICK OWENS

"In days gone by, there was a fair and a pub, a public house, at Arney Bridge.

"And there had to be a fight at the end of the fair. If I had an ashplant, I'd go over and tap you, and they'd all be into it. Ah, there were some good ones. They were rough long ago. People are more civilized now. In a sense.

"The fair was had one day every month. It was away in the evening, four or five in the evening, that the sport would have to rise. Everyone carried his stick. They had to be ready for it: you couldn't go without it."

HUGH NOLAN

"In them days cattle wasn't of such value. There was lots of cows around every house, but it was principally to supply milk and butter for the men that were at the brick-making and the turf-cuttin.

"I'll tell you what used to be: there used to be a fair on the tenth of every month in Enniskillen. Cattle wasn't very valuable, except the poor men had them. But the prices were small.

"Generally the calf that'd be born in the springtime, that calf would be sold before Christmas to have money for the season. And the price of that calf would be three, four, rarely five pounds.

"Before the creamery, all the milk they had to spare, they would thicken it and churn it. And any butter was left that was worthwhile, they would store it, salted, in a butt. That was made be the cooper. It was wooden and had wooden hoops, do ye see. And the churn, it was made be the cooper.

"It was as good a trade as what the motor mechanic would be today.

"And then the creameries started then, and that put an end to the whole business.

"Well, every Tuesday you would carry your butt of butter to Enniskillen. And there would be butter buyers, do ye see, in Enniskillen that would buy it by the pound.

"If ye couldn't fill a butt, your butter would be sold in the shops for a very low figure.

"Do ye see: the best lookin cow walkin, and her at the calf, would get you twelve, maybe fourteen pounds, and the neighbors would say you did well. And very few occasions there would be a twenty-pound cow. If you heard of a cow bringin twenty pounds and you at the fair that day, you'd be goin to see her. Oh aye. For a twenty-pound cow was a wonder.

"They would call that a Twenty-Pound Cow."

Slapbrick   HUGH NOLAN

"At one time the brick-makin was the industry of the country. It was all the material they had for buildin, do ye see.

"In later years the factory brick, it came along and it knocked out the slapbrick altogether.

"And later then the blocks come along.

"I don't think there was any slapbrick made in this country since the decade between nineteen and twenty and nineteen and thirty. It was inside of that decade that the last slapbrick was made in this country. No. I'm wrong now. There was a few cases where men wanted some brick for their own use. Aye, there was a man the name of Monaghan and his father made a kiln of brick in nineteen and thirty-nine. That would be the last brick that was made about this country. That was for his own use, do ye see, but as an industry the last of it would be in the twenties.

"The men that used to work at it are all dead and gone.

"Do ye see: brick clay was all through the country. And it was a big industry in Sessiagh, Rossdoney, them townlands in the vicinity of the Arney River.

"Them all had small farms that was in the brick industry. The larger ones didn't do so much of it unless they wanted to build something for themselves. They didn't adopt it for a livin.

"But the small farmers: it was principally be that they lived."

MICHAEL BOYLE

"I'm sure you've seen the stands of a few old kilns.

"There's a farm belongin to a man the name of Monaghan along the Rossdoney Road there. He made brick. There's the stand of an old kiln there.

"Well, the McBriens made brick. But the stand of their kiln's been drawn away."

"The day of the buildin, the day of the puttin them into the kiln was called the *crowdin*. They were crowded then, do ye see. That used to be a great day longgo. That we used to draw them in on the horses. There would be three or four horses, and there'd be a man drawin with every horse. Well then, there'd be a man out in the field and he'd be takin off this thatch and burnin it up carefully and puttin it to the one side and helpin the boys to build the *carts*.

"And they come in then, and—oh, it twas a big day's work; it took nine or ten men to be at it.

"And then a man would come in and he'd start on his lone and he'd pick two brick.

"We'll say I was here and you were there—generally the brick passed through about three or four hands. I was in the cart, we'll say, and I pitched two brick. And you catched them in your two hands. And you pitched them on to the next man. And the next man catched them and he pitched on to the next man, and the next man catched them and he pitched them on, till they went to the man, what they called, the crowder.

"And he was down, the same as he was buildin on a wall, only he had no mortar, do ye see."

HUGH NOLAN

"A day's crowdin was always a fair amount of sport. It was a great pastime for young lads.

"You and I would be drawin the bricks from the stack to the kiln, and they delighted in the pitchin of the brick, two at a time."

HUGH PATRICK OWENS

"My flesh crawls whenever I walk where they made the brick. I've tried to explain it to my children, but they can't understand.

"There's no work now so cruel.

"That was brutal, slavish work. And it was blood money came from it."

THE PEOPLE

HUGH NOLAN

"Young people got tired of brick-makin. It was hard work. And they took a notion to emigrate.

"And all these small pieces of land was sold. And some one man come to own it all."

The Man Who Would Not Carry Hay

JAMES OWENS

"The brick that built this house was made down there below. And the only transport they had was a creel on your back. Carried them up on a creel.

"Now you imagine all the brick that's in this house—to carry them in a *creel* on your *back*.

"They had no other way.

"And they used to carry the hay in on their back.

"There would be a man out in the field and that was his job: tyin up. He tied up the load for ye, *put it on your back*, do ye see, and away you went. Of course there might be five or six of them at this now.

"Well, there was only one horse cart in this country.

"It was down at the Ford there.

"And this man went this day to put in hay.

"He says, I'm goin to carry no hay and a horse standin up in the stable doin nothin.

"*Strike*. He went on *strike*; he went on strike.

"And they put the horse in the cart and they drew in the hay.

"Well, that ended the carryin of the hay.

"Imagine a horse standin up in a stable, and a cart, and carryin the hay on your back. Now didn't they do foolish things?"

111

William Quigley
MICHAEL BOYLE

"Well, there was a man lived in our country, William Quigley. He'd be an uncle of Paddy Quigley's.

"Well, he was a big, stout lump of a fearless man, and he was afraid of nothin.

"He wouldn't ask better than—any place he heared there was a *ghost*—someone'd tell him, So and such a one seen a ghost, such a place. Well now, says he, I must go till I see it.

"And he'd go away at night, in the middle of the night, to see would he *see* the ghost.

"And he *never* seen it.

"Aye ◊. That was the kind of him, you know.

"Well then, if he cut his hand—there's many's the one that cut their hand there—knock a lump of skin off it—he'd get a needle and a thread, and whatever kind of nerve he had, he could sew his hand with the needle and thread. He *often* done it.

"And *often* done it.

"Aye indeed.

"There was one time,
         he was doin somethin with the donkey and cart.

"The donkey bogged, you know, went down in the soft ground.

"And when he was gettin the donkey pulled up,
              some part of the cart,
              catched him be the shin,
         and tore a big lump of skin out of the shin,
              ah, that length.

"And he took a barber knife out of his pocket.

"And he cut off a lump of skin and threw it away.

"And got a needle and thread and put two or three stitches in it.

"And he hit it a rap of his fist,
   and he says:
      Ye'll be the tidier out of that.
"Aye, he was a great character altogether, this Quigley, a very powerful man."

Stories   HUGH NOLAN

"It was the usual thing that used to happen by the fireside, the ceilis that used to be longgo: one man would tell somethin, then another man would tell something forenent that, and it would go on around, and that's what they'd spend their night at. And then there'd be a discussion on whose pant was the best one.

"Well, the people used to come along for to get a number of these stories, for to judge which of them would be the best to tell if they were in some company.

"They used to analyze it from beginning to end and judge for themselves which story was the best, do ye see.

"Someone would propose this round of storytellin. Then if there happened to come strangers along, the natives would be watchin to see what stories that these men would give.

"But that has died away altogether in this country. The younger generations are not interested in it—from the radio and television came along."

"The way it is: the greatest stories, sure, they're all composed; they're all fiction.

"Somebody made them up.

"And isn't it a very smart person, man or woman, that can frame a tale? It's wonderful, you know.

"It's wonderful talent to be able to picture a long hot one and then fill it up, line by line. Oh now, it's wonderful.

"Well, do ye see, the way it is, it takes a person to be gifted in that line to do that. There's a gift attached to it, do ye see.

"Well, they're the same type of people as these authors that can compile a story there that you read out of a storybook or out of a newspaper, do ye see.

"These ones that can compile these short funny stories, they'd be the same type.

"Well, do ye see, an educated person with that gift, they could write away without ever—they'd be writin out of their head, do ye see—aye, whatever was in their head. But the other man that would tell these jokes and short stories, they mightn't have the education for to write, but they had the gift at the same time. The same gift. Aye.

"Well, it's very hard to explain how that gift comes about. But there's alot of people endowed with it, both educated people and uneducated people.

"And, whatever, it's surely a gift, because the uneducated man or woman, if they're given to that, they could come out with the same discourse durin the tellin of this as what one of these writers would.

"And, they mightn't know themselves the meanin of the words that they were usin, but they knew that they fitted in this tale that they were tellin.

"You see, the way it is with alot of these ones—the George Armstrong, John Brodison, or Hugh McGiveney type—they'd think of makin a poem or makin up a story. Well, they'd take a lock, first and foremost, at a certain group of words, and if it was a poem that they were goin to make, they'd judge, could you put that into verse. Well then, it would be the same with a story; they'd just judge, would this go well for the listener, would I be fit for to make this that it would carry away the listener or that there'd be a joke in it for them, do ye know. Aye."

John Brodison

HUGH NOLAN

"John Brodison. He was a Cavan man. He came to Fermanagh to work, and he settled down in it, and first he lived away down below Lisgoole.

"When I started goin to Enniskillen first he was livin down there. And then awhile at Arney and finally he came to Bellanaleck in the latter end."

MICHAEL BOYLE

"At a time there was a terrible plague of rabbits in the country—ah, they destroyed all the vegetables.

"So John Brodison had a wee cabbage bed anyway,
            and his was safe.

"And someone asked him how did he manage to keep his cabbage bed safe from rabbits.

"I had no bother, he says.

"I went down to the quarry, he says,
        and I riz a wee cart of stones,
        and I put the stones around them, says he,
        and I went to Cathcart's shop there,
            and I bought a pound of pepper,
        and I dusted the stones, he says, with the pepper,
        and the rabbits came and they started to sneeze,
            the pepper got into their noses,
            and they started to sneeze,
        and they knocked their brains out ◊
            agin the stones, sneezin ◊.

"Aye.

"Aye: they knocked their brains out agin the stones.

"Aye, he was one star. He was one star, this Brodison."

HUGH NOLAN

"Oh many a good story John told.

"There was one time there was a terrible windstorm.

"It was—ah, it lasted the most of a day and a night, do ye know.

"The wind started, we'll say, tonight, about twelve or one o'clock, do ye see, and then blew on to mornin, and then it continued durin the followin *day*. It would be the followin evenin when it settled.

"So anyway, there was another man lived convenient to John. He was the name of McGrath. Oh, he was a great star.

"So a few days after this storm, the two met on the road, and of course generally in this time of year in Ireland when two people would meet there, they'd be talkin about the nice day it was at this time of year. That would be in the *winter* season. That bes a thing that nearly everyone talks about: the *good* day, that there'd be no rain or no wind; they'd be commentin on how nice a day that was for that time of *year*.

"So anyway their conversation was to that effect and then it came round about this storm that had passed.

"So John Brodison says:

"Well now, he says, it was as bad a storm as *I mind*.

"Ah now, there must've been alot of harm done
        through this country.

"Now I was standin
    in the door, he says, at about seven o'clock
        that night.

"And it had been blowin *all* the day
    and blowin from the night afore
    and it was still, it was still blowin.

"And there went a haystack by

116

and a man on the dass of it.

"Oh, says this McGrath man, I seen worse that night
        because I was comin down from Bellanaleck Cross
        and I met a byre comin from Arney
                and the cows all loose through it.

"Aye ◇.

"Weren't they a pair of smart men that could go on that way?

"Do ye see: this McGrath man, he composed that while the other man was tellin him about what he seen, do ye see. He just composed that, do ye see. He had it ready when the other man was done. To beat him out.

"Beat him out, do ye see, that was the idea.

"Oh aye, surely.

"This was a wonderful place for witty bids and good yarns and bein able to compose a thing, do ye know."

George Armstrong HUGH NOLAN

"This George Armstrong, he lived in a little house in Gortdonaghy. His house was down at the foot of the hill. Missus Cutler's house, do ye see, would be away up on the top of the hill. Well, you'd have to come down towards the north to come where his house was.

"When he left it, a nephew got the farm, and that man built a house on the Arney Road and sold the farm to a neighbor. Before he left he built a temporary iron house.

"He was a wonderful storyteller, a wonderful storyteller of things that there was nothing *about*.

"He was tellin about:
        there was one mornin he was sittin at the fire.

"He heared a flock of wild geese.

"And, do ye see, there was guns goin in this country in days gone by. They were *muzzle loaders*.

"Ye charged them with powder and shot, and you put in the powder first. And you put a piece of paper in after it, and you had a *ramrod*, and ye pushed that away down with the end of the ramrod.

"So then you put in the shot after, and a piece of paper on the top of it. And you pushed it down.

"So then there was a cap on the gun and when you pulled the trigger there came a spark out of the cap that set the powder afire and it blew the shot away out.

"Them was what they called muzzle loaders.

"Well, he minded this mornin that he had no shot.

"So he ran

and he put powder into the gun,
and he pushed it down with the ramrod,
and he left the ramrod in the gun,
and he ran to the fire,
and as the wild geese was crossin the house,
he fired.

"The ramrod went up,
and it stuck in three of their necks;
three of them fell down on the roof of the house,
dead.

"The ramrod stuck in their necks ◇.

"Aye ◇.

"He was in Australia
in his young days.

"And he was doin the best, makin plenty of money.

"But there started a disease, they call it cholera. It's goin in foreign countries *still*, I think.

"So,

he was very bad with it,

and he thought he was goin to die.

"Finally he started to mend anyway, and he got in the latter end that he was able to get to his feet, and
get out.

"So he made up his mind that he'd get back to Ireland,
if he could atall.

"He hadn't very much money. It wasn't hard in them days for to pay your fare on the *high seas*.

"But anyway, he started.

"And he discovered that the ship that he was travelin in:
that there was a cow's grass of land, he said,
of the best land ever he set his eyes on,
in the ship,
and there was a rood of the best turf bog
that ever any man put a spade in.

"So anyway, he made his way on anyway and I think it was in Derry he landed.

"So he made his way to Enniskillen,
and he got out on the platform,
and there was a weighbridge on the platform,
and he got up on the weighbridge,
and he was three pound weight.

"Aye ◇.

"So he was seven mile from home at the time.

"And he seen that was all for him, frail and all that he was—was to walk home; he had no way—there was postcars in them days, but, ah, you wanted to have a lock of shillins about you, you know, for to hire one of them.

"So he started anyway.

"So he come on, and at that time there was a railroad crossin on this Derrylin Road, down near the end of it; it's gone now; you wouldn't see hardly any track of it, only a bridge across the Sillees River.

"So anyway the train was comin,
 and he just took a notion he'd count his money,
  he was sittin on the back of the ditch,
 and he searched his pockets,
  all he had: thruppence.
"Train passed anyway,
 and he got to his feet again,
 and he come on,
  and finally,
   finally he made his way,
    so he landed at the house.
"There was no noise atall off his step;
  he was that light.
"He came along without any noise and when he arrived
at the door,
  the mother was doin something at the fire,
   and she never found him
    till he spoke.
"So when she turned round and seen him,
  aw she nearly lost her life at the appearance of him.
"There was a wee basket hangin to a purline that was in
the kitchen,
  that she took down the basket,
  and she put him into the basket,
   and she put a white cloth over him,
   and she left him up at the fire.
"So the rumor went out about the country that George
was returned, that George was home.
"So there was alot of people arrived there the next day,
for to see him and have a talk with him.
"And when they came in there was no sign of George
about.
"So anyway some of them says:

"Well, we heard that George was home and we just came to see him.

"Oh, *here he is,* says the mother. He's home yesterday evenin.

"And some of them says to her, Where is he at the present time?

"Oh, he's not far away, says she.

"So she went and lifted up the wee basket,
     and took the cloth from over him ◇,
     and they looked in it ◇.

"That was all the chat you got out of George; he wasn't able to talk.

"It was pants like that you know, pants like that he used to tell."

James Quigley   HUGH NOLAN

"There was a man,
     he lived there just,
          on this side of the parochial house.

"John Maguire, he's livin there now. It's when you're goin up the Arney Road there, the house is on your right-hand side. There's television aerial that you'd see there, apparatus. He's John Maguire that lives there now.

"But there was a man lived there before him, he was James Quigley.

"And he was great, great rant.

"I heared him tellin about
     there was some man and
          he was gettin it very tight for money.

"And he tried all ways of makin money, but it was a failure.

"But he heared of such a thing as sellin yourself to the Divil

for a length of time.

"But you'd have to go with him when this time would expire.

"But durin the period between you'd made the bargain with him,

and between the time that you'd have to die,

you'd have plenty of everything,

plenty of money,

and everything that you wished for.

"He'd supply it.

"So anyway, this man he got in contact with him anyway,

and he sold himself to him for a number of years.

"So he got terrible rich.

"Everything went well with him.

"But anyway, the time expired.

"So he used to *meet* with him

on different occasions, do you know.

"And Ould Nick, as they called him, used to tell him everytime how long that it had to go now, till he'd have to be goin *with* him.

"But anyway in the middle of his whole riches he got downhearted.

"And he started to worry.

"So,

he didn't know how he'd get rid of him,

or how he'd get the bargain broke.

"So it was givin him terrible trouble.

"And he put things before the Ould Nick that he didn't think that he'd *do*

in the line of,

ah, supplyin money to houses of worship,

and things like that, do ye know.
"Everything was a failure.
"So *anyway* in the long run,
    he got totally downhearted.
"And the wife noticed him,
    she got afraid that, well,
    that he was gettin near his death or
    that he was goin to loss his senses.
"So she got around him anyway. She never had knew anything about this bargain that he had made with the *Playboy*
    till that.
"So she sifted on
   and sifted on
     and sifted on at him,
   till she got him to tell her,
      to tell her all.
"So.
"Oh now, he says, I have no hope, he says,
   but he says, that he *has me.*
"No, she says.
   He hasn't ye *yet*, she says.
"So when they started the bargain first, there was one time that the Divil came along and he had a wee drum with him and a pile of sticks.
"And he gave the man the wee drum.
"And he says,
   Anytime ye want me, he says,
     give a roll on this drum.
"So anyway that was the way he used to notify him when he wanted to get anything *done.*
"So says the wife to him,
   He hasn't ye *yet.*

"Aw now, says he, how do *you* know;
    I know his decision.
"There's one thing, says she, that ◊
    if you ◊
    put it before him, she says,
    he'll not give into it, or he'll not do it.
"And what is that, says the man.
"Well, says she, ◊ the next time, she says, when he comes
along
        tell him
        that you want him
        to do *one* thing,
    and it's the last thing that ever you'll ask him to do,
    and that if he does it, you're willin to go with him.
"And what is it, says the man.
"*Ask him*, says she, *to make all lawyers honest men.*
"He *up to his feet and he got the drum*
        and he *rolled.*
"Oh aye ◊.
"Aw now, there *never was a roll of a drum heard as far in the
world.*
"So it was no time till the lad appeared.
"What do ye want now, he says.
"Well, he says, I *want* ye to do a thing, he says, and it's
the last thing, he says, that ever I'll ask ye to do,
        and if ye do it, he says,
        I'm willin to go with ye, he says.
"*What* is it, says he.
"I want ye, he says, to make all lawyers honest men.
"HA!
"Oh, now, he says,
    there's *women*, he says,
        at the back of this, he says.

"It's a thing, he says, I'll never do, because if I did I wouldn't be long before I wouldn't have a coal on me hearth.

"Give me that drum, he says,
        because, he says,
            I'm *finished* with you ◊.

"So he got rid of him.

"That was the last of him."

Hugh McGiveney   MICHAEL BOYLE

"Ah, I mind Hughie well.

"He was a small-sized man, and he had a kind of a crouch. He walked with a kind of a crouch, with his two hands behind his back.

"And he was a nice man, a nice discoursed man, you know. Aye a great wit. In fact, he was the wit of the whole country, Old Hughie.

"Oh he was a great man.

"He had an old donkey; he called it Fanny Ann.

"Fanny Ann.

"And he used to go to the bog for a load of turf, two creels, do ye see. Straddle and mats. There was a pin stickin up out of the straddle, do ye see, and a creel fixed on every pin. And he used to go off to the bog every day, him and Fanny Ann, for two creels of turf, a load of turf.

"I remember McGiveney.

"He used to go to all haystacks.

"They used to put hay in big ricks before the haysheds was built.

"He went to all haystacks, you know, and there used to be great bids with him. It was a great day at a hay stack longgo: There'd be a jar of porter and a good big feed, and then the ould boys would get a mug or two of porter to put them in humor.

"And it would be the greatest fun ever you seen
                              with these old boys.

"It would be great entertainment.

"He was a great man at dressin one of these big ricks of hay, do ye see, keepin it in order. A funny man.

"Ah he was a great lad, a great wit.

"Oh, he was a terrible wit.

"Oh, he made several poems, you know, about things. He was a great wit, do ye see, he made several bits of songs about things that happened.

"Ah, he was a great lad, Hughie McGiveney. He was a great wit, you know terrible clever man, do ye see.

"We'll say that it was nowadays, that the same facilities was in education. If he had the same facilities in them days as there is today, he'd have been a counsel. Oh yes. He was as quick as lightnin in his answers, do ye see. He had two brothers in America. I never met them of course (they were gone before my day), but they turned out great men in the States.

"There was one of them a John McGiveney, another Owen. They turned out great, great men in the States.

"And of course, you see, he had only a small wee home there, a wee small bit of land. And they sent home the full of a hat of money to him, do ye see. There wasn't a great livin on that couple of cows' grass of land. He got piles of money from them, and they never came back to visit him, I think. But indeed, they didn't forget him anyway.

"He would have been a great man if he had of got the chances that there is now. He was terrible quick. He wouldn't have to mass a thing until he'd have the answer out, do ye see. Great bids in him, do ye see.

"He was a great character.

"Ah, he was a great star.

"He was a great star."

THE PEOPLE

"In days gone by, there used to be what they called *joins*. It would be a gatherin up—there'd be an announcement made round the neighborhood: Well, we're goin to a *night* in such a house, do ye know. And we're gatherin up a lock of bobs to get a drop of drink and maybe *tea* and *bread*. So men used to put in their bit. That happened every year for years and years.

"There was some one particular man took charge of the money. It was spent on the spree.

"Every man would give in a subscription, and when there'd be a bit of money all gathered up, some two would go to *Arney*, and they'd buy a go of—it was generally *whiskey* in them days. Whiskey was *cheap*. A lock of half-pints of whiskey.

"Ye'd get a half a pint of whiskey in them days for fourteen pence in the old money.

"You paid so much and I paid so much and Johnny Boyle paid so much and Francy Corrigan paid so much, and, well, it was generally men that was *drinkin*, men that was drinkin.

"So they'd get right boozed. And this man Bob Flynn, he used to start makin the wills of all the men round the country, drawin up their wills on the table.

"So now, he'd leave the land to such a one; he'd leave so much money to such a purpose, all to this.

"Oh, he used to make a whole go of wills, you know. Every man in the house, he made their will.

"He was a great man for makin a bit of a speech. Comical kind of man.

"He lived in a small house, the next place to Quigley's, in Drumbargy.

"I heared a man tellin about
    bein at one of these functions.
"And this Quigley, he was a very hot-tempered man.
"And he was great fire when he'd get drunk, you know.
"But this night Hugh McGiveney was in it.
"And Christie, as his name was, he got real drunk.
"So anyway, Hughie was sittin at the fire and he looked towards the dresser.
"And there was a wee pot just in the front of the dresser.
"So Hughie got up to his feet and
    he went down and
    he lifted up the pot and
    he looked into the pot and
    he looked under the pot and
        where the pot *was*,
    and he looked round the whole dresser.
"Some of them says to him: What are you lookin at Hughie?
"Well, he says, I seen the Devil goin into that pot.
"So man ◊, Christie was sittin in the corner,
    and Christie up to his feet,
    got aholt of the pot and he out
    and ◊ he broke the pot into bits agin the wall ◊.
"Well then, ah, it used to last until near mornin."

MICHAEL BOYLE

"Hughie McGiveney used to tell a yarn, used to say— this whole district of the country was Ballymenone, and Saint Patrick, he says, never came to Ballymenone when he was preachin the gospel in Ireland.

"He came to the shore,
over at Inishmore,
and he shook the staff,
over at Ballymenone.
"He says,
Aw, Ballymenone,
you are there, he says,
I'll not bother callin to see you atall.
I know you're there.
"Well, he never was in Ballymenone, he said.
"He came to Inishmore, he says,
and he shook his staff over into Ballymenone ◇."

HUGH NOLAN

"Ah now, Hugh McGiveney was a wonderful, intelligent man. Well, he had brothers and they were the same. They went to America. They could make poems.

"It's a general rule that a race like that finally dies out altogether, because I've seen a couple of instances in this country. The people that was celebrated for some thing, they died out in the finish. Aye."

"Hugh McGiveney he made that song about the Ford of Biscuits:

I see the plumes of Duke's Dragoons
Before Belturbet town.

"Ah now, he made up another few songs, but I'll tell ye: he never wrote them down, and then when he died, the songs were lost, you know. Aye, they were lost.

"Ah, he was a great artist."

Songs

HUGH NOLAN

"Well, I'll tell you the way it used to go.

"You and I would meet on the road, maybe some night during the winter. And you had Saturday night left out for to go ceiliin, or you had Sunday night. Well, if you were around the locality together, couple of mile, you'd pick out where would be the best place to go for a night's singin. Or where would be the best place to go for a night's storytellin. That was the way it used to be organized.

"So you'd arrange on goin to a certain place. A certain man, if he didn't live there, he used to ceili there. Then we'd tell a couple more, Francy Corrigan and Paddy McBrien, where we were goin, and they'd go *too*.

"And that was the way. Everyone would sing a song, or tell a story. That was the way that the custom was kept *alive*."

"There was men at that stage in history and they'd have a song and they could sing it, but they mightn't be more than able to write their own name, do ye see.

"And that was the cause of alot of songs goin out of existence. Because the people that had them wasn't fit for to *write* them down, and then nobody else bothered about it.

"They'd listen to a person singin, and they'd enjoy the song, but the thought never occurred to them that it would be a good job to get that song wrote down, do ye see."

"There was alot of people in days gone by, and they were interested in puttin anything that happened, puttin it into *verses*."

Maxwell's Ball MICHAEL BOYLE

"It's a song that was made on a *ball* that was in the island of Inishmore: Maxwell's Ball.

"The poet was kind of unknown, I think. There was three or four of them, I think, three or four of them at the composin of it. There was a fellow the name of McCourt. He lived in the island of Inishmore, do ye see, and he was at the composin of it: Mickey McCourt. He lived in the island of Inishmore. And he was another rare boy, this Mickey McCourt. He had alot of songs. He had alot of songs, and he had some of his own composition, but he had others then, do ye see, that he *picked up*. But at any rate that's not the story.

"This Maxwell's Ball, it was in a house the name of Maxwell's in Inishmore. And of course a gooddeal of the lads of our country went over to it. So anyway, there was a song made. And the song was made on a girl and a fellow, do ye see. And the girl she left the fellow durin the ball, do ye see. They were sweethearts, do ye see, and durin the ball she left him and went away with another fellow, so he was in a terrible state, of course.

"So anyway, didn't some of the lads make up a song about it anyway.

"The song run:

One night when I was courting,
    I went unto a spree.
With polished boots and fancy socks,
    I was dressed up to a tee.
With tommy cuffs and buttons,
    and a collar white and tall,
I went to meet my Nora
    that night at Maxwell's Ball.

They were there in all persuasions,
in numbers great and small.
They hailed from Carna Cara
and from Tonyloman too,
And from sweet old Montiagh's shores,
their numbers weren't few.
They braved the dangers of the waves;
they came both one and all
To patronize the gathering
that night at Maxwell's Ball.
The ladies they were charming
and beautiful to view,
And some were dressed in Blarney tweed,
and more in navy blue.
While some, they wore tight jackets
to make their waist look small,
Till I really thought they'd split in two
that night at Maxwell's Ball ◇.
It was there I spied my Nora
unto her I did say,
Just come into the dining room
and we will have some tea.
Right willingly she came with me,
she was ready at the call.
Oh, she et the dose, I paid for all
that night at Maxwell's Ball.
But then my pleasures ended,
and my heart felt sore and sad,
When I found me Nora had left me
I went distracted mad.
I rambled up and down the room
on Nora I did call,
Till I found her on her suitor's knee

that night at Maxwell's Ball.
While some did laugh and more did chaff,
while I sat in suspense,
Thinkin how I lost my Nora
likewise my eighteen pence.
And everywhere I go, the boys do on me call:
Or did you get your Nora
tonight at Maxwell's Ball?
But now the ball it's ended,
and I have one word to say:
It's never go in for courting
till the ladies takes the tea,
For if you do, I'll tell to you,
they'll make you very small.
They'll set you runnin mad like me
that night at Maxwell's Ball ◇.

"That's the poem now. That's the song the boys made up.

"Mickey McCourt and Hugh McGiveney, they both helped with it. But they bid to be clever boys because they were supposed to make up the song that night and sing it at the ball.

"They did. That's what I believe.

"There were a couple that was at the ball told me that.

"An old man that's dead and gone longgo, he told me that they composed it at the ball, made it up at the ball. That's what I heard.

"That was a true song. That all happened.

"My mother—God be good to her—she remembers it happenin. And I was talkin to fellows that was at it. I was talkin to old men—they were old men in my day—that was at the ball, that remembered it all.

"And I knew the men that made it. I knew the men that made it all right."

The Star of Ballymenone   MICHAEL BOYLE

"Well, there was another song composed in our District. I mightn't have it right, but I think I have a gooddeal of it right.

"It was made on a pair of lovers in our country.

"Aye, the boy's name was McHugh, and the girl's name was Barclay. And they were natives of the country. And they were goin together—they were married afterwards, but they were married in the States; they didn't get married in Ireland.

"So I think he was killed in the First World War with the American army, as far as I heard.

"But however, I'll make an offer to tell you all I know of it anyway.

"Well, the start of it is—

"Well, our whole district of the country was called Ballymenone. Well, this lady was called the Star of Ballymenone. She was a fine-lookin girl.

"But anyway:

As I rambled out one evenin,
    it being in the summertime,
To view the pleasant Arney brooks
    that do like silver shine,
As I walked along the Arney Road,
    I thought the country grand,
With long brick hacks and big turf stacks,
    all through The Holy Land.
Tonyloman looked so gay
    with its hills of shamrock green,
And many breeds of wild fowl
    fly up from Inishkeen.

The wild goose and the mighty swan
*   and other birds are known;*
It was a glorious sight to see their flight
*   over the hills of Ballymenone.*
As I followed on the wild birds' flight
*   right to Lough Erne's shore,*
And to the strand of an island,
*   they call it Inishmore,*
While walking down long Polly's Brae,
*   a young couple there did roam,*
And the fair one's name was Maggie,
*   the Star of Ballymenone.*
They both were of an equal stamp;
*   she held tight by the hand.*
No wonder why his darting eye
*   might well entice*
*   the Star of Ballymenone.*
This couple fair, they did compare
*   about a song to sing:*
I will my Jim, she did begin,
*   with heart so keen,*
*   the Maids That Wore the Green.*
And she says, My Jim, I must go home.
He gave consent and home he went
*   with the Star of Ballymenone.*
To all entrusted true lovers,
*   this couple I'll recommend.*
My advice to you, young Jim McHugh,
*   is never for to roam,*
But for your bride, take by your side,
*   she's the Star of Ballymenone.*

"That's the song.

"Well the composer was unknown. It never was known right who made it. Because I think it caused a kind of a wee bit of bad humor like. I think it did, as far as I heard. So the composer was kind of unknown; it never was known who made it anyway.

"There's not too much about it, but as far as I used to hear like—I didn't know the people atall. I know friends of theirs all right. I know friends of theirs to the present day, but I didn't know them. Well, they were gone away to the States before my time.

"But it's a lovely thing. I think that's it all. I might've dropped out wee bits in it, here and there, but that's the song, that's The Star of Ballymenone."

Charlie Farmer   MICHAEL BOYLE

"I'll tell ye, there was another great poet. They called him Charlie Farmer. He was from Kinawley, up that country. P could tell ye more about him.

"He made a bit of a rhyme one time on a policeman that was stationed in the ould barracks at Mackan. He was the name of Reilly, and he was a great man for runnin after the ladies. But he summonsed this Charlie Farmer for somethin, ah, some wee simple event, you know, and Charlie Farmer made a bit of a poem about him:

> There's ten thousand girls in Ireland,
> To put the question mildly,
> But if there was ten thousand more,
> There's not enough for Reilly ◊.

"A bit of a rhyme, do ye see.
"I only seen him occasionally. He was a small size man, a

small size man. Oh, I seen *Charlie*. But I never heard him sing like, or I never heard much of his poetry, only wee bits here and there, but he made alot of songs, do ye see. Oh aye, he did. P might know more of them because he lived convenient to him, do ye see, and he might be fit to have some of them."

PETER FLANAGAN

"Charlie Farmer.

"It twas him made that song, The Men of Ninety-Eight. And he was only a wee unsignified-lookin poor wee fellow with a wee chubby beard. And he lived all alone.

"And that was one of the songs that he made."

A hundred years has passed and gone since Irish men they stood
On the green hillside of Erin and for freedom shed their blood.
The Irish race is called upon for to commemorate
Those brave United Irishmen who died in Ninety-Eight.

Then: hurray for the flag, the dear old flag of green.
And hurray for the men who beneath its folds is seen.
Hurray for those heroes we now commemorate:
Those brave United Irishmen who died in Ninety-Eight.

Tyrannical oppression reigned supreme throughout our land,
And trampled on the the people's rights till they could no longer stand.
Our gallant soldiers up they sprung against Saxon's crown and hate,
And swore they'd save their land or die, the men of Ninety-Eight.

(Chorus of the second stanza)

The standard of the green unfurled while cheers does blend the air
That waved now proudly over the men of Wexford and Kildare.
And Father Murphy blessed our arms and bravely led us on.
We'll ne'er forget old Suchatharoon. Hurray for Father John.

137

(*Chorus*)

They fought and died for Ireland, oh how they died in vain.
Are we content to live as slaves beneath a tyrant's chain?
Ah no, my boys, while Irish blood through Irish veins does flow,
We're ever ready at the call to strike another blow.

Then: hurray for the flag, the dear old flag of green.
And hurray for the men who beneath its folds is seen.
Hurray for those heroes we now commemorate:
Those brave United Irishmen, who died in Ninety-Eight.

"Oh, he made alot of songs. That one is commemoratin the men of Ninety-Eight for their gallantry. He was very intelligent, and he saw the trouble his country was in and he composed these songs so people wouldn't forget."

"He made several songs. But unfortunately, I haven't them.

"He made several songs. It twas him made that Kinawley."

Come to Kinawley, that historic place,
That once has been the pride and the home of our race,
Before the invader, he dared show his face
In our sanctified home in Kinawley.

Come to Kinawley and there take your stand
In the struggle for freedom we'll join heart in hand.
An Irish Republic is all we demand
And we'll have nothing less in Kinawley.

Our own saintly curate, we'll greet with a smile.
He loves every inch of our beautiful isle.
He talks with his people the same as a child,
And he's loved by us all in Kinawley.

(Chorus of the second stanza)

Our priest and our people together they'll stand
With their backs to the wall, and they'll fight for our land.
In liberty's cause they will join in the band,
And they'll drive out the foes from Kinawley.

(Chorus)

Come to Kinawley and there you will see
The flag of a nation, it floats from a tree.
Stand under its folds if you want to be free,
And shout up Sinn Fein in Kinawley.

(Chorus)

Come to Kinawley and pray at the shrine
As of holy Saint Naile, it's in olden time,
Before the Normans and Saxons committed the crime
For to plunder our old homes in Kinawley.

(Chorus)

While begging from England we were but old fools.
While trusting their statesmen, they made us ould tools,
But now we are out for to kill British rule,
And to bury their corpse in Kinawley.

Come to Kinawley and there take your stand
In the struggle for freedom, we'll join heart in hand.
And an Irish Republic is all we demand
And we'll have nothing less in Kinawley.

"And then he made another one—political too. He made one about the fight here on the Border.

"He started it off:"

The great League of Nations is now in despair,
And war it is looming again in the air,
And an order has came from Belfast to prepare
For a bloody campaign on the Border.

We thought when the rule of the Kaiser had ceased
That Europe was in for the blessings of peace,
But a hero named Cooper has taken his place,
And he threatens to march on the Border.

The law and the treaty, this hero defies
In a speech that he made on the Twelfth of July.
He shouts, No surrender, we'll conquer or die
In a bloody campaign on the Border.

His army composed of the A B and C,
Old men and cubs not the height of you knee.
It would be well worth your while for to go there and see
This rebel brigade on the Border.

I would advise Mister Cooper at home for to stop,
For to stay at his desk or remain in the shop,
For some of these snipers this hero might pop,
And the battle would be lost at the Border.

When he goes to the Border to make his attack
I would venture to say he would never come back,
Except his remains be sent home in a sack
To be buried away from the Border.

"Well, poor Farmer, he was void of an air. The creature hadn't an air. He could make the song all right. And there was a fellow beside him, he was McCaffrey, John McCaffrey. He was only young of course. Farmer was maybe in his fifties.

And he would put the airs to his songs.

"Well, I was very sorry when Charlie Farmer died, because I was gettin to like him at the time. Me and him was pretty great.

"So the poor fellow passed out of it. And this younger man that used to put the airs to his songs, he got married and him and the woman went away to Scotland, some part of Scotland. With the result I never could contact him. But anyway and everyway, not many years ago I met him, and he was a dead old man.

"He used to sing these songs of Farmer's in the country house dances, all little dances. They used to run an annual dance there in Kinawley for the upkeep of the parish school. He used to sing them whole songs, and that's the only way that I got in contact with them songs, Kinawley and the other few bits.

"Well, I was very pleased to meet Johnny McCaffrey, and I thought that he was the man that I knew thirty years before. But, I met him and shook hands with him and chatted on. I suppose you can sing, says I, some of Farmer's songs. No, I wouldn't mind, he says, one of them. He was old, he was, well seventy-five, and then he went away, and he died shortly after. All was lost.

"All was lost except the ones that I know. But he made, I suppose, a good deal of songs more than that."

"It's a pity Charlie Farmer wasn't in a district where there was singers. I wasn't just a native of it at that time. A house was wantin, and we happened to go temporarily to this house beside Charlie Farmer. But he was on the way *out*.

"And he had quit composin. And he had quit everything you might say. The poor wee fellow.

"You wouldn't think—if you seen him and he was a very

unsignified-lookin type of person. The modestest wee fellow and he had a wee beard comin down just like a wee nib of a pen, you know.

"He was the nice tiny wee fellow.

"And every word you'd ask him, he'd say,

"Aye.

"That's a good day, Charlie.

"Aye.

"You would think that he knew nothing—that type of person.

"But if he got into talk he could use the best grammar ever you heard. And I don't know where he got his education. Really. Sure, I was stupid and, of course, when you're young like that you don't look at the full details of history.

"It was a great sorrow, and often I would cry about the loss of his songs.

"He was a historian as well as a poet. He was both."

"It's a pity. All the funny people's gone.

"He made great songs, Charlie Farmer.

"But there wasn't a singer in the townland where Charlie Farmer lived. And even if you're not a singer out in public. There's plenty of people, you know, are very good singers but wouldn't sing out in public.

"Well, if you even had them people in your district where Charlie Farmer was, for example, there wouldn't be a song of Charlie Farmer's but it would be alive today.

"Wherein, there wasn't a singer in this townland where Farmer lived, only this boy, McCaffrey. And there was plenty of young fellows. But they were deaf to music as a stone. Well then, the man that can't sing or hasn't much music in him, hasn't much interest in learnin a song or takin it up or knowin the value of it. There was only that one man that took a great interest in Charlie Farmer, and some of his script is down in Belfast, that was Eddie Anderson.

"Eddie Anderson was the man that knew the value of Charlie Farmer.

"He could see that day comin.

"And he done the same thing you're doin, gettin these songs down. You're doin a great thing. No one knows the value of men like you. It brings great honor and credit to a nation. There's alot into what you're doin.

"But you haven't a man in ten square miles around here, and I could extend it further, that knows the value of a man like Charlie Farmer.

"Well, it won't be very long before it will be extinct or gone completely, that no one will ever get a grip of it. No.

"It's regrettable that it hadn't been saved or preserved and kept alive. Now there's no one in Tiravally now or three miles round, or five miles, that would know one haet about Charlie Farmer, that he existed atall. That's the way.

"You want plenty of men like you. It's a pity there's not more. There's no one has the wee remnants of Charlie Farmer except meself. Unfortunately, I didn't see him early enough in life.

"In the present generation, if you're not fit to get a grasp on his poetry, it will die out. He made many, many songs. He made that one on the Border. And he made one on Trimble, the Reporter editor. And he made one about Willie Oliver, and one on the Molly Maguires, the A O H, that's the Ancient Order of Hibernians. And he made another on a policeman named Reilly. And he made that one on John Greene and the donkey race.

"He made some very funny songs. There's no doubt about it. Farmer was the last word in poetry. He was. He was a wonderful man."

"He was a lone man. He had a sister. She went to America when he was young. And he remained on. And I think he got into poor circumstances. He had a small wee farm. She came back, and she redeemed the place for him.

"He was an easy-goin person that never had any ambition, you know, for workin or risin to great heights or anything like that, you know.

"He still held on.

"And of course age got in on him.

"And he had a big red cow. And he was bringin her, you know, what they call, to the bull.

"And she was a pet cow. And the poor fellow was walkin that way, just in front of her with the halter, and the cow was comin behind, and what did she do, only rise up behind him and put him down. And that was that. They had to get the doctor.

"He never riz.

"He was brought home then, and he lay in bed and he went to hospital, and that was the end of poor Charlie.

"That's what happened poor Charlie.

"And there was far worse poets in this country that has been recognized very much and got great publicity and all. He never—he had no ambition. At that time of course there was no wireless and no television. In fact there was no—music and song in these later years, it has been revived up terribly in this country. If Charlie Farmer had been alive now he'd have featured amongst the greatest of our Irish poets. That's namely, Thomas Moore and James Clarence Mangan, and all of them; you've heard tell of them all. Ethna Carbery. Charles Kickham that sings, I live beside the Anner. Well, Charlie Farmer was as good as any of them. Oh, he went very deep into—very deep-meanin songs.

"He composed, in fact—ah, I didn't hear the half of

them. I believe he had a stack of songs and then the people that got his wee place at his death, they didn't know the treasure, nor the value; they burned stacks and stacks and stacks of his good poetry.

"Well, he has died now without any recognition."

NOTES

When Lady Gregory went folklore-collecting in Galway, she sought fairy stories, mysterious tales of supernatural encounter, but her notebooks filled as well with tales of historical events, which she gathered into *The Kiltartan History Book*, published in 1909. In its expanded second edition (London: T. Fisher Unwin, 1926), her *History Book* remains the great Irish collection of historical legends. She said she had the right to praise it because it contained no word of her own. I praise it as a major anticipation of the modern concern with folk history. In it we discover the people's own view of their past.

Though folklorists in Ireland as elsewhere favor the imaginative over the factual, the unusual over the commonplace, many of the fine anthologies of Irish folktales include historical legends. Sean O'Sullivan's *Folktales of Ireland* (Chicago: University of Chicago Press, 1966), with its excellent survey of Irish scholarship by Richard M. Dorson, is an exemplary collection. And Sean O'Sullivan has added *Legends from Ireland* (London: Batsford, 1977). Northern folklorists have given us fine collections of stories from Ulster, notably T. G. F. Paterson, *Country Cracks: Old Tales from the County of Armagh* (Dundalk: W. Tempest, Dundalgan Press, 1945); and Michael J. Murphy, *Now You're Talking . . . Folk Tales from the North of Ireland* (Belfast: Blackstaff Press, 1975).

The rationale for the poetic transcription of "prose" narratives is set forth clearly by Dennis Tedlock, "On the Translation of Style in Oral Narrative," in Américo Paredes and Richard Bauman, eds., *Toward New Perspectives in Folklore* (Austin: University of Texas Press, 1972), pp. 114–33; and Dell Hymes, "Discovering Oral Performance and Measured Verse in American Indian Narrative," *New Literary History* 8 (1976/77): 431–57.

Good introductions to the variety of song—locally called "political" or "patriotic"—that dominates the south Fermanagh repertory can be found in Patrick Galvin, *Irish Songs of Resistance* (New York:

Folklore Press [c. 1960]); and Georges-Denis Zimmermann, *Songs of Irish Rebellion: Political Street Ballads and Rebel Songs, 1780–1900* (Hatboro: Folklore Associates, 1960).

The great introduction to Irish rural culture is E. Estyn Evans, *Irish Folk Ways* (New York: Devin-Adair, 1957). No one, I believe, has caught the feel of life today in the Ulster countryside better than John Montague in his volume of fine verse, *The Rough Field* (Dublin: Dolmen Press, 1972). The conditions of farming existence in Fermanagh west of Upper Lough Erne are set out in John M. Mogey, *Rural Life in Northern Ireland* (London: Oxford University Press, 1947), chap. 3; and Leslie Symons, ed., *Land Use in Northern Ireland* (London: University of London Press, 1963), pp. 238–39. The texture of life in Fermanagh at the turn of the century was captured in fiction by Lough Erne's own novelist, Shan F. Bullock, especially in *Irish Pastorals* (New York: McClure, Phillips, 1901) and *The Loughsiders* (New York: Dial [1st pub. 1924]).

I have written two other books on the people who live on the hills along the Arney. The first, *All Silver and No Brass: An Irish Christmas Mumming* (Bloomington: Indiana University Press; Dublin: Dolmen Press, 1975), described the community's Christmas drama. The second, *Passing the Time in Ballymenone: Culture and History of an Ulster Community* (Philadelphia: University of Pennsylvania Press, 1982), attempts a full ethnography of daily life and contains this book's texts embedded in analysis. Below I list this book's topics in order of appearance. For each I give the author and the date of recording. Most texts were taped, but some were taken from dictation. Since dictation is less satisfactory than tape-recording, I have followed each date with a letter—"t" for taped, "d" for dictated—so you can evaluate it. Then I provide a brief note, but for fuller comment and richer annotation I refer you to particular chapters in *Passing the Time in Ballymenone (PTB)*.

1. SAINTS

SAINT PATRICK: Hugh Nolan, 8/23/72t. Mr. Nolan's description of Saint Patrick's entourage tallies with that given by the Four Masters in their great work of 1636: John O'Donovan, ed., *Annals of the Kingdom of Ireland, by the Four Masters* (Dublin: Hodges, Smith, 1854), 1:134–41. Muirchu's *Life* is translated by Newport J. D. White, *St. Patrick: His Writings and Life* (New York: Macmillan, 1920); book 1, chaps. 15–18, tells the story of the Paschal flame on the Hill of Slane. James Carney has clearly and cogently weighed fact and fiction and assessed conflicting scholarly opinion in *The Problem of St. Patrick* (Dublin: Dublin Institute for Advanced Studies, 1973). *PTB*, chaps. 6, 28.

SAINT NAILE: Peter Flanagan, 8/27/72t. Saint Naile established Kinawley, Cill Naile, in Fermanagh and succeeded Saint Molaise at Devenish in 564, according to the Rev. J. E. Canon McKenna, *Devenish (Lough Erne): Its History, Antiquities and Tradition* (Enniskillen: Fermanagh Herald, 1931), p. 90. Saint Naile's story is told by Eamon Anderson of Kinawley in manuscripts in the archives of the Department of Irish Folklore, University of Dublin College at Belfield: Irish Folklore Commission (IFC) vol. 891 (1942): 407; and IFC 948 (1943): 201–2. *PTB*, chaps. 6, 28.

ISLANDS OF SAINTS AND SCHOLARS: Hugh Nolan, 8/23/72t; Peter Flanagan, 8/27/72t; Hugh Nolan, 6/16/77t. Saint Columbanus was born in Leinster around 543 and he studied with Saint Sinell, who founded a monastic school on Cleenish Island in the middle of the sixth century: Mary Rogers, *Prospect of Erne* (Enniskillen: Watergate Press, 1971), pp. 101–3; John T. McNeill, *The Celtic Churches: A History, A.D. 200 to 1200* (Chicago: University of Chicago Press, 1974), p. 158. *PTB*, chaps. 6, 28

SAINT FEBOR: Hugh Nolan, 8/23/72t. John O'Donovan tells the tale of Saint Febor in a letter dated November 6, 1834, included in the Rev. Michael O'Flanagan, ed., *Letters Containing Information Relative to the Antiquities of the County Fermanagh, Collected During the Progress of the Ordnance Survey in 1834–35* (Bray: privately published, 1928), pp. 54–55. *PTB*, chaps. 3, 4.

SAINT COLUMCILLE: Hugh Nolan, 6/11/77t. The life of Columcille (521–597) was written late in the seventh century by Adamnan,

IRISH FOLK HISTORY

his successor at Iona. Adamnan tells of the battle of Cúl Dreimne, two years after which, in 563, Columcille sailed for Scotland, and he tells of the Saint's return to the Council at Druim Ceat in 575, where he prevented the abolition of the bardic order: Alan Orr Anderson and Marjorie Ogilvie Anderson, eds., *Adomnan's Life of Columba* (London: Thomas Nelson, 1961), pp. 224–25, 315–17. Adamnan does not relate the dispute over the book. That tale was told by Manus O'Donnell in the sixteenth century: A. O'Kelleher and G. Schoepperle, eds., *Life of Columcille Compiled by Manus O'Donnell in 1532* (Urbana: University of Illinois, 1918), pp. 176–201. The great early seventeenth-century Irish historians tell Mr. Nolan's story: O'Donovan, ed., *Four Masters*, 1:192–95; and Geoffrey Keating, *General History of Ireland*, trans. Dermod O'Connor (Dublin: James Duffy, 1861), pp. 356, 370–88. O'Donnell, the Four Masters, and Keating all report some version of the proverbial judgment "The cow and the calf ought always to go together" (Keating, p. 376). Seán Ó Súilleabháin provides a text in Irish from the oral tradition as number 88 in his excellent collection of religious tales, "Scéalta Cráibhtheacha," *Béaloideas* 21 (1951–52). *PTB*, chaps. 6, 28.

2. WAR

THE FORD OF BISCUITS: James Owens, 11/14/72t. John O'Donovan discusses the name Beul Atha na mBrioschadh in a letter of 1834 in O'Flanagan, ed., *Letters of the Fermanagh Ordnance Survey*, pp. 63, 65, and in a footnote to the *Four Masters*, 6:1952.

THE TAKING OF RED HUGH O'DONNELL: Hugh Nolan, 6/16/77t. Mr. Nolan's account of the capture and escape of O'Donnell (1571–1602) agrees closely with that in the early Irish biography: Paul Walsh and Colm O Lochlainn, eds., *The Life of Aodh Ruadh O Domhnaill Transcribed from the Book of Lughaidh Ó Clérigh*, Irish Texts Society 62 (Dublin: Educational Company of Ireland, 1948), pp. 4–33. *PTB*, chaps., 8, 28, 31.

THE BATTLE OF THE BISCUIT FORD: Hugh Nolan, 6/11/77t; Michael

150

Boyle, 10/26/72t. The story of the Siege of Enniskillen and the Battle of the Ford was written in the early seventeenth century by the Four Masters and by Sir James Perrott: O'Donovan, ed. *Four Masters*, 6:1940–45, 1948–55; Herbert Wood, ed., *The Chronicle of Ireland, 1584–1608, by Sir James Perrott* (Dublin: Stationery Office, 1933), pp. 70–71, 75–81. Red Hugh O'Donnell did not command the Ulster forces at the battle, though his men were there, led by Hugh Maguire and Cormac, the brother of Hugh O'Neill. Michael Boyle said that Hugh McGiveney's song was printed in the *Fermanagh Herald*, but the paper's editor, P. J. O'Hare, kindly wrote in response to my query that he doubted it. *PTB*, chaps. 8, 28, 31.

BLACK FRANCIS: Hugh Nolan, 8/30/72t; Peter Flanagan, 8/30/72t. Paddy Tunney, the singer from north Fermanagh, tells a story of Corrigan's race and leap comparable to Mr. Flanagan's, though heightened toward the fabulous, in *The Stone Fiddle: My Way to Traditional Song* (Dublin: Gilbert Dalton, 1979), p. 32. *PTB*, chaps. 3, 4, 5, 28.

MACKAN FIGHT: Hugh Nolan, 8/23/72t; Michael Boyle, 10/26/72t; Hugh Patrick Owens, 8/11/72d. Thomas Owens, who died about 1940 at the age of eighty-three, was Hugh Patrick Owens' father. Late in his life he composed at least two poems dealing with Mackan Fight. I quote his "A Tourist Visit" from papers which Mr. Owens generously let me copy. In his excellent history, *The Fermanagh Story* (Enniskillen: Cumann Seanchais Chlochair, 1969), Peadar Livingstone provides the history of the battle and quotes a text of the most common of the "Mackan Fight" songs (pp. 161–66), of which Michael Boyle recites a part. *PTB*, chaps. 9, 28.

THE TOSSING OF THE CHAPEL AT SWANLINBAR AND "THE SWAD CHAPEL SONG": Peter Flanagan, 8/27/72t; James Owens, 11/14/72t; Owney McBrien, 11/26/72t. Eamon Anderson gives the history of the event and a text of the song in Michael J. Murphy's manuscript, IFC 1695 (1965): 74–80. Anderson attributed the song to Mary Byrne. I heard it attributed to the author of "Mackan Fight," and I heard "Mackan Fight" credited to three different men named Maguire who lived near Kinawley at the end of the last century. *PTB*, chaps. 9, 28, 31.

THE BAND: Joseph Flanagan, 8/26/72d; Michael Boyle, 10/26/72t. The band engaged in two battles, both narrated to me by Mr. Boyle, both remembered in song by Hugh McGiveney. Alex Mc-Connell of Bellanaleck tells the stories and gives the songs in his manuscript, IFC 1403 (1955): 18–25. *PTB*, chaps. 10, 28.

THE BROOKEBOROUGH RAID AND "SEAN SOUTH": Ellen Cutler, 8/14/72d; Gabriel Coyle, 8/30/72t. Sean South and Feargal O'Hanlon were killed in a raid on the R.U.C. station at Brookeborough, County Fermanagh, January 1, 1957, which is described by Livingstone, *The Fermanagh Story*, pp. 382–86. Mr. Coyle's long second stanza blends the second and third stanzas of other renditions, such as that in *Songs of the Irish Republic* (Cork: C.F.N., 1972), p. 4. *PTB*, chap. 10.

THE FLAG THAT FLOATS ABOVE US: Peter Flanagan, 8/13/72t. *PTB*, chap. 2.

Mackan Fight

Played by Peter Flanagan on the tin whistle. Transcribed by Lore Silverberg.

The Swad Chapel Song

Sung by Owney McBrien. Tune transcribed by Julie Górka.

You — gen - tle — mu - ses — pray _____ ex - cuse — me for my in - tru - sion on learn - ing's wing. And in - spire my — gen - ius — you bards — and — sa - ges; my coun - try's — prai - ses — I mean to sing. Tra - di - tion teach - es with - out con - sul - ta - tion, and bless - ed Pa - trick was first — and all, To Pope Cel - est - ine — and prune — our — vi - ne - yard called In - is - ill - gi - e or the Vir - gin — Shore.

Sean South

Sung by Gabriel Coyle. Tune transcribed by Julie Górka.

It was on a — drea - ry New Years' Eve as the shades of night fell down, A ____ lor - ry load of ____ vol - un - teers a - pproached a bor - der town; There was men from Dublin and — ____ from Cork, Fer - man - agh, and Ty - rone, But the lea - der ____ was a Lime - rick man Sean South of Ga - rry owen.

NOTES

3. THE LAND

DAYS OF THE LANDLORDS: Hugh Patrick Owens, 8/11/72d; Hugh Nolan, 10/27/72t and 11/15/72t; Peter Flanagan, 10/25/72d. The Land League's victory is narrated by Elizabeth R. Tooker, *Readjustments of Agricultural Tenure in Ireland* (Chapel Hill: University of North Carolina Press, 1938), pp. 42–49; and analyzed by Samuel Clark, *Social Origins of the Irish Land War* (Princeton: Princeton University Press, 1979). *PTB*, chap. 18.

MRS. TIMONEY'S REMARKABLE WALK: Michael Boyle, 11/25/72t; Hugh Nolan, 12/18/79t. *PTB*, chap. 18.

THE FAMINE: Hugh Nolan, 10/27/72t. Cecil Woodham-Smith recounts the course of the Famine in *The Great Hunger: Ireland, 1845–9* (London: Hamish Hamilton, 1962). *PTB*, chap. 19.

MR. MCBRIEN: Michael Boyle, 10/28/72t. Alex McConnell of Bellanaleck took down a version of this story from Mr. Boyle's uncle: IFC 1403 (1955): 26–27. *PTB*, chap. 19.

CASTLE GARDEN: Peter Flanagan, 7/9/72t. A fragment of this song appears in John Meredith and Hugh Anderson, *Folk Songs of Australia* (Sydney: Ure Smith, 1979), pp. 149–50. *PTB*, chap. 32.

SKIBBEREEN: John O'Prey, 7/23/72t. This song has often been printed and recorded: Richard L. Wright, ed., *Irish Emigrant Ballads and Songs* (Bowling Green: Bowling Green University Popular Press, 1975), pp. 52–63, 682–83. Hugh and Lisa Shields, "Irish Folk-Song Recordings, 1966–1972," *Ulster Folklife* 21 (1975), no. 368, report texts from the field, including an Irish translation. *PTB*, chap. 32.

LOVELY ERNE'S SHORE: Owney McBrien, 11/26/72t. *PTB*, chaps. 9, 32.

A LOVELY COUNTRY: Hugh Nolan, 7/14/72d. The "comical man" is Hugh McGiveney. *PTB*, chap. 14.

The Flag That Floats Above Us

Sung by Peter Flanagan. Tune transcribed by Lore Silverberg.

The slave may bend in ab-ject fear, And he may hug the chains that bind him, And the cow-ard may run his base ca-reer, No flag of free-dom find him. But while a-bove us floats the flag, Of green and or-ange blen-ded, No tyrant, nor no knave, its folds shall drag While our stout arms de-fend it.

Skibbereen

Sung by John O'Prey. Tune transcribed by Lore Silverberg.

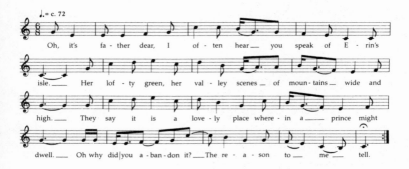

Oh, it's fa-ther dear, I of-ten hear you speak of E-rin's isle. Her lof-ty green, her val-ley scenes of moun-tains wide and high. They say it is a love-ly place where-in a prince might dwell. Oh why did you a-ban-don it? The re-a-son to me tell.

THE FERMANAGH SONG: Martin Crudden, 11/20/72t. Most people credited this song to Bryan Gallagher, headmaster of St. Aidan's High School in Derrylin. In 1981 Master Gallagher generously replied to my letter of inquiry saying the song "has been attributed to many people in the locality and many have claimed authorship of the words and music. The only thing I know for certain is that I did not compose either." *PTB*, chap. 14.

4. THE PEOPLE

LIFE: Hugh Nolan, 10/27/72t, 12/18/79t; Ellen Cutler, 11/13/72d; Rose Murphy, 7/18/72d; Hugh Nolan, 8/30/72t; Hugh Patrick Owens, 8/11/72d; Hugh Nolan, 7/14/72d. For the social arrangement of work in other Irish communities: Conrad M. Arensberg and Solon T. Kimball, *Family and Community in Ireland* (Cambridge: Harvard University Press, 1968), chaps. 1–4, 12; John C. Messenger, *Inis Beag: Isle of Ireland* (New York: Holt, Rinehart & Winston, 1969), chap. 2; Rosemary Harris, *Prejudice and Tolerance in Ulster* (Manchester: Manchester University Press, 1972), chap. 5; Robin Fox, *The Tory Islanders* (Cambridge: Cambridge University Press, 1978), chap. 5. *PTB*, chaps. 12–16, 20–26.

SLAPBRICK: Hugh Nolan, 8/1/72d; Michael Boyle, 11/20/72t; Hugh Nolan, 7/14/72d; Hugh Patrick Owens, 8/17/72d; Hugh Nolan, 8/1/72d. Alex McConnell of Bellanaleck describes the local brick-making industry in his manuscript, IFC 1403 (1955): 111–15. *PTB*, chaps. 21, 25.

THE MAN WHO WOULD NOT CARRY HAY: James Owens, 11/14/72t. *PTB*, chap. 17.

WILLIAM QUIGLEY: Michael Boyle, 11/11/72t. *PTB*, chap. 2.

STORIES: Hugh Nolan, 6/22/77t, 6/16/77t. *PTB*, chap. 2.

NOTES

Lough Erne's Lovely Shore

Sung by Owney McBrien. Tune transcribed by Julie Górka.

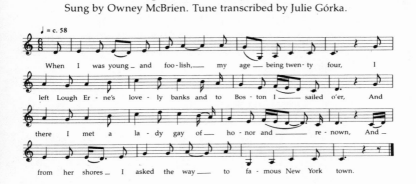

When I was young and foolish, my age being twenty four, I left Lough Erne's lovely banks and to Boston I sailed o'er, And there I met a lady gay of honor and renown, And from her shores I asked the way to famous New York town.

The Fermanagh Song

Sung by Martin Crudden. Tune transcribed by Lore Silverberg.

Good people all, on you I call, and this song I will sing for you. Twas written with a loving hand, each word is fond and true. It's all about Fermanagh, and the first thing I will do Is take you to the Hangin Rocks near the village of Belcoo.

NOTES

JOHN BRODISON: Hugh Nolan, 11/15/72t; Michael Boyle, 11/25/72t; Hugh Nolan, 11/28/72t. In *The Stone Fiddle*, p. 88, Paddy Tunney tells a tall tale that, though not the same as Michael Boyle's, is comparable. Mr. Nolan's story of the Big Wind would fit under motif X1611 in Stith Thompson's *Motif-Index of Folk Literature* (Bloomington: Indiana University Press, 1955–58). *PTB*, chaps. 2, 15.

GEORGE ARMSTRONG: Hugh Nolan, 11/8/72t. The first of the two stories Mr. Nolan strung together to tell about Armstrong, The Lucky Shot, is type 1894, normally elaborated by Mr. Nolan and others into type 1890D in Antti Aarne and Stith Thompson, *The Types of the Folktale* (Helsinki: Suomalainen Tiedeakatemia, 1961). Seán Ó Súilleabháin and Reidar Th. Christiansen, *The Types of the Irish Folktale* (Helsinki: Suomalainen Tiedeakatemia, 1964), pp. 325–26, show that this tale from the Munchausen canon, so common in America, is known in Ireland, though not well known. Another Ulster text: Murphy, *Now You're Talking*, p. 136. The second, more important story, George Armstrong's Return, incorporates motif X924. *PTB*, chap. 2.

JAMES QUIGLEY: Hugh Nolan, 11/8/72t. This is a humorous reworking—perhaps by Quigley himself, said Mr. Nolan—of a variant common in Ireland of Aarne-Thompson type 1187, the classic text of which was given by Samuel Lover in *Legends and Stories of Ireland* (Dublin: W. F. Wakeman, 1834), pp. 141–56. *PTB*, chap. 20.

HUGH MCGIVENEY: Michael Boyle, 10/26/72t; Hugh Nolan, 11/22/72t; Michael Boyle, 11/25/72t; Hugh Nolan, 6/11/77t, 6/22/77t. There is a story that Saint Patrick never went to Kerry. He came, looked, blessed, and hurried on: Mr. and Mrs. S. C. Hall, *Ireland: Its Scenery, Character, &c* (London: Hall, Virtue [1850]), 1:243; D. R. McAnally, *Irish Wonders* (Boston: Houghton Mifflin, 1888), p. 55. *PTB*, chaps. 2, 8, 26, 32.

SONGS: Hugh Nolan, 6/22/77t, 11/15/72t. *PTB*, chaps. 2, 9, 32.

NOTES

The Men of Ninety-Eight
Sung by Peter Flanagan. Tune transcribed by Lore Silverberg.

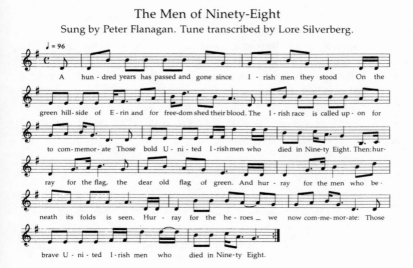

MAXWELL'S BALL: Michael Boyle, 11/11/72t. Alex McConnell of Bell-analeck provides a text of the song in his manuscript, IFC 1403 (1955): 61–64. *PTB*, chaps. 2, 32.

THE STAR OF BALLYMENONE: Michael Boyle, 11/11/72t. Though not the same song, this is related to "Greenmount Smiling Anne," no. 182 in this vast collection of folksongs from Ulster: Gale Huntington, ed., "Sam Henry's 'Songs of the People,'" unpublished manuscript, pp. 470–71; which is also found in James N. Healy, *The Mercier Book of Old Irish Street Ballads* (Cork: Mercier Press, 1967), 1:273–74. *PTB*, chap. 32.

CHARLIE FARMER: Michael Boyle, 11/25/72t; Peter Flanagan, 8/6/72t, 12/18/79t, 12/17/79t, 11/12/72t. "Kinawley" was written to draw people to a big Sinn Fein rally in the small Fermanagh border town of Kinawley during the 1916 period. Farmer wrote

159

"The Bloody Campaign of the Border" after reading an editorial in the *Impartial Reporter* that threatened resistance to the idea of redrawing the Border to cede parts of south Fermanagh to the Republic of Ireland. Eamon Anderson, the Eddie Anderson Mr. Flanagan mentions, lists Farmer among other Kinawley poets in his manuscript notebook deposited in the archive of the Ulster Folk and Transport Museum (pp. 47, 52), and he gives one of Farmer's songs, "Willie's Harvest Home," in IFC 1695 (1965): 85–88. *PTB*, chap. 32.

Kinawley

Sung by Peter Flanagan. Tune transcribed by Lore Silverberg.

Come to Kin - aw - ley, that his - tor - ic place That once has been the pride and the home of our race, Be - fore the in - va - der, he dared show his face In our sanc - ti - fied home in Kin - aw - ley.

A NOTE ON THE ILLUSTRATIONS

The head on the cover comes from one of the stone figures from White Island in Lower Lough Erne, photographed in August 1978. These sculptures date between the ninth and eleventh centuries; for them see Helen Hickey, *Images of Stone: Figure Sculpture of the Lough Erne Basin* (Belfast: Blackstaff Press, 1976), pp. 34–52; fig. 14(c) shows the entire statue. The drawing on the title page presents the view north from Gortdonaghy Hill, photographed in July 1972. The detail of the Soiscél Molaise was drawn from Françoise Henry, *Irish Art During the Viking Invasions (800–1020 A.D.)* (Ithaca: Cornell University Press, 1967), plate 58; and Máire and Liam de Paor, *Early Christian Ireland* (London: Thames and Hudson, 1978), plate 64. Saint Molaise, founder of the monastery on Devenish, sentenced Columcille, the mate of his soul, to exile. The detail of the O'Craian tomb in Sligo Abbey was drawn from photographs taken in June 1977. Talk about Sligo Abbey led to Hugh Nolan telling the story of "The Battle of the Biscuit Ford" included in this book. The Croziers' home, viewed from the scene of the first episode in Mackan Fight, was drawn from photographs taken in March 1976. Mr. Nolan's portrait was drawn from sketches made in his home and from photographs taken in December 1979.